Frederick Gard Fleay

Introduction to Shakespearian Study

Frederick Gard Fleay

Introduction to Shakespearian Study

ISBN/EAN: 9783337055721

Printed in Europe, USA, Canada, Australia, Japan

Cover: Foto ©ninafisch / pixelio.de

More available books at **www.hansebooks.com**

Collins' School and College Classics.

INTRODUCTION

TO

SHAKESPEARIAN STUDY.

BY

F. G. FLEAY,

AUTHOR OF 'THE SHAKESPEARE MANUAL.'

LONDON AND GLASGOW:
WILLIAM COLLINS, SONS, AND CO.
1877.

PREFACE.

As I have already published one book on Shakespeare, I am bound to anticipate the objection—Why write another that goes in some measure over the same ground? The answer is not far to seek. A book was needed for younger readers who have not power, and for popular readers who have not time, to master critical questions concerning Shakespeare, and who yet are desirous of acquainting themselves, to some extent, with the results of those investigations that have been made. I have been repeatedly asked to publish, in a separate form, the portions of my *Manual* which are independent of any subjective theories. This is not, however, what I have done. This book has nothing in common with the *Manual* but what is common to all general treatises on, or critical editions of, Shakespeare. It is partly an introduction and partly a supplement to the larger work, yet I trust complete in itself.

The book differs from the previous one in the following particulars :

1. It is meant for younger readers, and a more popular, not so critical a public; although there are in it things that I trust may be useful even to the latter.

2. It only extends to the end of Shakespeare's life, 1616, instead of embracing the whole history of the Elizabethan and Jacobean drama.

3. It omits all such topics as metrical tests, controverted questions, lists of actors, and matters essential to the more advanced student, but a hindrance to the beginner. On the other hand, it contains entirely new matter to the extent of

three-fourths of the book, and the rest has been altogether re-written, not condensed from the *Manual*. I may specially mention, among the new matter, the full accounts of the doubtful plays, the lives of contemporary dramatists, the excerpts on grammar founded on Schmidt's *Lexicon*, the account of the alterations to which plays were subject, the chapter, on the presentation of plays, founded on P. Chasles, the tables compiled from the accounts of revels at court and Henslow's *Diary*, and the final chapter on the connection of Shakespeare's plots. But neither this nor its predecessor are supposed to contain everything which a student requires, although this does, I trust, contain all that is needed for popular readers or young students, apart from the ordinary annotations on the text; and the larger work is meant to embrace all that, in addition to such books as Schmidt's *Lexicon* and Abbott's *Grammar*, will be needful for some considerable time of study.

Wherever there is a discrepancy in dates, etc., between the *Introduction* and the *Manual*, the *Introduction* may be generally trusted. The differences are due to the stereotyping of the *Manual* by the publishers without my knowledge, and the consequent perpetuation of the errata, a list of which was sent them by me in August 1876. I believe that the great care of the printers, and my further experience in correcting for the press, have kept the *Introduction* nearly free from 'printer's errors.'

To the friends who have formerly aided me by their encouragement to further work, I wish now to add the names of Dr Ingleby and the American Shakespearians, Messrs Crosby and Furness; to the critics who have so cordially welcomed me, I tender my sincere thanks, in trust that their encouragement may produce in me still better and more useful work.

F. G. FLEAY.

33 AVONDALE SQUARE, OLD KENT ROAD, S.E., 1877.

CONTENTS.

CHAPTER I.
                                              PAGE
HOW DID SHAKESPEARE LIVE? 9

CHAPTER II.
WHAT POEMS AND ROMANTIC PLAYS DID SHAKESPEARE WRITE? 17

CHAPTER III.
WHAT HISTORIES OR CHRONICLE PLAYS DID SHAKESPEARE WRITE? 30

CHAPTER IV.
WHAT OTHER PLAYS HAVE BEEN ASCRIBED TO SHAKESPEARE? 40

CHAPTER V.
HOW SHOULD SHAKESPEARE BE READ? 47

CHAPTER VI.
WHO ACTED PLAYS IN SHAKESPEARE'S TIME? . . . 53

CHAPTER VII.
WHERE WERE PLAYS ACTED IN SHAKESPEARE'S TIME? . 55

CHAPTER VIII.
WHO WERE SHAKESPEARE'S CONTEMPORARIES? . . . 57

CHAPTER IX.

AUTOBIOGRAPHY OF A STAGE PLAY, ... 69

CHAPTER X.

HOW WERE SHAKESPEARE'S PLAYS REPRESENTED? . . 72

DOCUMENTARY APPENDIX.

I. ABSTRACT OF SHAKESPEARE'S WILL, 25TH MARCH 1616, ... 75

II. THE FAMILY OF SHAKESPEARE, ... 76

III. ENTRIES AT STATIONERS' HALL, . . . 78

IV. LIST OF QUARTO EDITIONS, ... 80

V. EXTRACTS FROM THE ACCOUNTS OF THE REVELS AT COURT, ... 83

VI. EXTRACTS FROM HENSLOW'S 'DIARY,' GIVING LIST OF PLAYS PERFORMED AT THE ROSE THEATRE, 1592-7, 88

VII. HENSLOW'S 'DIARY' CONTINUED, 1597-1604, . . 91

VIII. ALLUSIONS OR SUPPOSED ALLUSIONS TO SHAKESPEARE BY CONTEMPORARIES, ... 104

SUPPLEMENTARY CHAPTER.

SHAKESPEARE'S PLOTS: HOW ARE THEY CONNECTED? . 111

INTRODUCTION

TO

SHAKESPEARIAN STUDY.

CHAPTER I.

HOW DID SHAKESPEARE LIVE?

WILLIAM SHAKESPEARE was the son of John Shakespeare of Stratford, and Mary Arden of Willmecote, who were married about 1557. This John Shakespeare had lived in Henley Street, Stratford, from 1552 at least. He was well-to-do and respected. He had copyholds of two houses, was a burgess, a member of the Stratford corporation, a dealer in gloves and barley. He had property in Snitterfield from his father, and in Willmecote from his wife; he became an affeeror or fixer of fines for the borough, municipal chamberlain, and member of the common-hall, in rapid succession.

On 26th April 1564, his third child and eldest son, William, was baptized at Stratford. Between this date and 1575, we find him lending money to the borough, making up the chamberlain's accounts, acting as alderman, high bailiff, and finally 'Magister Shakespeare, chief alderman.' He had also bought two houses in Henley Street.

William was probably, during the latter part of this period, at Stratford Grammar School, under Curate Hunt or Thomas Jenkins.

But in 1577, maybe from poverty, maybe from living out of the town on lands newly acquired at Bishopton and Wilcombe, John Shakespeare attended the meetings of the corporation irregularly: half his borough taxes were remitted. In 1578 Asbies, his wife's inheritance, was mortgaged to Edmund Lambert, who was also security for him to Roger Sadler for a debt of £5. He was excused from a poor-rate of 4d. a-week. In 1579 a levy on him for soldiers was left unpaid. About this date William most likely left school at some thirteen or fifteen years old, and became a lawyer's clerk, or at any rate entered on some occupation for his livelihood.

At the age of eighteen, he married Anne Hathaway, seven years his senior. The marriage-bond was dated 28th November 1582. Fulk Sandells and John Richardson, farmers of Stratford, became bound in it for the lawful solemnisation of the marriage, with once asking of the banns. On 26th May 1583, six months after, Susanna, William's first daughter, was baptized; and on 2d February 1585, his twin-children and last, Hamnet and Judith.

A John Shakespeare (but there were three of this name in Stratford) was distrained on 19th January 1586, a writ issued against him, and he deprived of his alderman's gown for not attending at the halls. Whether this was William's father or not, our dramatist left Stratford for London about 1585, and began his career there in poverty. There is great reason to believe that the old tradition of his holding horses at the theatre door during performance time, has a basis of fact; and it is almost certain that he very soon obtained employment in the company of Lord Strange's players, as an actor.

There were other companies at this date, namely—the Queen's, Pembroke's, Admiral's, Chapel Children, and Children of Paul's. The chief dramatic writers were Lilly, Greene, Peele, Marlow, Kyd, and Lodge. The theatrical world then, as in most times, was disturbed by angry rivalries and bitter quarrels. We cannot trace Shakespeare in these distinctly till 1589, when the advent of firebrand Nash in London kindled a conflagration among them. Peele and Marlow on one side, and Greene on the other, had already had their quarrels; but then two distinct camps were formed, Nash and Greene leading the one, Peele and Marlow the other. Shakespeare belonged to the latter, but took little if any part in the quarrel, though he was bitterly attacked by both Nash and Greene. In this same year, 1589, he probably made his first attempt at dramatic writing in the comic portions of the *Taming of a Shrew* in conjunction with his friend Marlow; but in 1592, Greene's allusions to him were still aimed at him as an actor, rather than an author, so that it is unlikely that he was generally known to have written anything at that date. John Shakespeare, meanwhile, was still in possession of his house in Henley Street, and in 1592 was described as a 'credible man' employed in making an inventory.

In 1592 Philip Henslow opened the Rose Theatre on the

Bankside, and one of the *new* pieces performed in that year was *Henry VI*. That this play was the same as that now known as 1 *Henry VI*, there is little doubt; and that Shakespeare's contribution at that time consisted of the episode of Talbot's son, John, in the fourth act, is highly probable. We have here the first appearance of Shakespeare as a dramatist, though only to the extent of vamping, or at most of aiding in writing a not very high specimen of historical drama. The authors of the rest of this play were Marlow, Peele, and perhaps Lodge. The theatres in the next year were closed on account of the plague; Lord Strange's company went into the country to play, and did not return to the Rose.

From this time forward, Shakespeare, though he did not leave his 'quality' of acting, is an acknowledged author as well. In 1593 he published his *Venus and Adonis*, and no doubt had produced one or two of his earliest recognised plays, *Love's Labour's Lost*, etc. But it will be more convenient to treat of these plays separately, and not to interrupt the regular narrative of his life by noticing them here, as their dates are still in many instances matters of dispute.

In 1594 Shakespeare published his second poem, the *Rape of Lucrece*. Both his poems were dedicated to Henry Wriothesley, Lord Southampton, to whom also the *Sonnets* (1-126) were, in my opinion, addressed in 1596. At this latter date, the early group of dramatists had almost disappeared. Greene had deceased in beggary; Marlow had been stabbed in a drunken brawl; Peele was dead or dying of a disgraceful disease. Shakespeare's disgust with the stage may be seen in the *Sonnets*. But we are anticipating. In 1594 Lord Strange's company became the Lord Chamberlain's on the death of Ferdinand, Earl of Derby. This company, with Shakespeare among them, acted before Queen Elizabeth at Greenwich, at Christmas in that year. This is our first positive notice of him as an actor. In 1596 the company was at the Curtain Theatre in Shoreditch. It probably settled there about that time, having previously been acting 'about the city of London'—among other places, for a few days at Newington Butts, under the management of usurer Henslow—and during the winters at the Crosskeys, Gracechurch Street.

On the 11th August, this year, Shakespeare's only son, Hamnet, was buried at Stratford; his sorrow as a father is shown in Act III, sc. iv, of *King John*. On the 29th December, his uncle Henry was buried; and Henry's wife, Margaret, on the following 9th February. But this break-

ing up of the family was succeeded by the establishment of
Shakespeare's fame as a dramatist; this death of his son by
the birth of his brain progeny. For on August 6th, the very
week of Hamnet's death, Edward White entered for publication the first play that Shakespeare gave to the press, *Romeo
and Juliet;* and this date may be fairly taken as the dividing
point between what are called his first and second periods.
From this time till 1600, every play he wrote was published;
as well as revisions of a few of those that were produced in
his first period. His name, however, was not put on any
title-page till 1598, but except on that of *Romeo and Juliet*,
it was never omitted afterwards.

In 1597 the application for a confirmation of a grant of
arms, made at the Heralds' College in behalf of John Shakespeare, was granted. In the same year, William had enough
money to buy of William Underhill the New Place in Stratford, once called the Great House. It was built by Sir Hugh
Clopton in the time of Henry VIII, and consisted of a messuage, with barns, gardens, and orchards. He was also assessed
on 1st October 1598 at £5, in the parish of St Helen's, Bishopsgate. In the same year, his parents filed a bill in Chancery
to recover Asbies from John Lambert, son of Edmund, to
whom it had been mortgaged in 1578. They alleged that
they had duly tendered money in release, according to agreement, but that the estate was nevertheless withheld from
them. In the same year, Francis Meres published his
Palladis Tamia, or *Wit's Treasury,* in which he not only
aided our chronological investigations by giving a list of the
twelve plays Shakespeare had then produced, but also showed
the estimation in which he was held by frequent mention of
his lyrics, elegies, comedies, and tragedies. Nor was the
influence of Shakespeare confined to literary matters. On
24th January 1598, Abraham Sturley wrote from Stratford
to Richard Quiney, Judith Shakespeare's future father-in-
law, in these words : 'It seemeth that our countryman, Mr
Shakespeare, is willing to disburse some money upon some
odd yard land or other at Shottery, or near about us. He think-
eth it a very fit pattern to move him to deal in the matter of our
tithes. By the instructions you can give him thereof, and by
the friends he can make therefore, we think it a fair mark
for him to shoot at, and not impossible to hit. It obtained
would advance him indeed, and would do us much good.'
The matter in question was a solicitation to Burleigh, Lord
Treasurer, to obtain an exemption from subsidies and taxes
for Stratford, and a grant of a portion of £30,000, set aside

INTRODUCTION TO SHAKESPEARIAN STUDY. 13

by Parliament for relieving decayed towns. There had been great fires there in 1594-5. Advance in wealth is also shown by the fact that he held corn and malt to the amount of ten quarters; only two others in his ward held as much. He sold stone to the corporation, and was looked to as a probable lender of £30 to Richard Quiney. About this time (1599), his sister Joan married William Hart, a Stratford hatter, to whom he was much attached.

To return to the theatre. In 1598 Jonson joined the Chamberlain's company, and produced *Every Man in his Humour*, in which Shakespeare acted; but in 1599, in his next play, *Every Man out of his Humour*, played by the Chapel Children, made a violent attack, not without provocation, on Marston, Dekker, and other contemporary poets. But he did not confine his attacks to them. He also attacked Burbadge, and, I think, Shakespeare. This raised a controversy which cannot be entered into here. It must suffice to say that it went on till 1602-3, when Jonson left the Chapel Children, came back to the Chamberlain's company, and produced his *Sejanus*. In this play Shakespeare acted, and it has been supposed that he wrote part of it; Chapman's, however, was probably the 'second pen' which aided Jonson in this play. The share that Shakespeare took in this controversy has never been fully shown. It is pretty clear, however, that he was called 'Deformed,' and 'Shadow,' if not other names. His feelings towards the Children players may be seen in *Hamlet*, II, ii, and an allusion to his name Deformed, and the plagiarism he was accused of, in *Much Ado about Nothing*, III, iii.

Meanwhile great changes had taken place in the theatres. In 1598-9 the Theatre was pulled down, and the building of the Globe commenced with the old materials. To this house the Chamberlain's company moved, and there all Shakespeare's plays, from 1599 onwards, were produced; that is, probably all that were not included in Meres' list. The theatre at Blackfriars, built in 1596, was let to the Chapel Children, who played there till 1603. The Revels Children succeeded them in 1603-4. The Fortune Theatre was also built in 1600, by Ned Alleyn; and the Admiral's company, who had played at the Rose since 1594, went to the Fortune in October 1600, leaving the Rose for the occupation of the Earl of Worcester's company.

In this same year, 1600, Shakespeare's name was put on the title-page of a play written for the Admiral's company by Munday, Drayton, Wilson, and Hathaway. This impudent forgery was the work of a piratical bookseller, T. Pavier, who in this year also published a surreptitious issue of *Henry V.* Whether in consequence of this or not, no quarto edition after 1600 of any of Shakespeare's works was issued with his consent. They were all thenceforth unauthorised by him or by the company. These piracies, however, show how his reputation was advancing : so do the ninety extracts from his writings in *England's Parnassus,* 1600, and the quotations in *Belvedere* and in *England's Helicon.*

In 1601 we find his name attached to a poem in R. Chester's *Love's Martyr, or Rosalin's Complaint;* and on 8th September, John Shakespeare's burial was entered in the Stratford register. At this date occurs the passage from the second to the third period of his works. This date is also marked by the only long journey of which we have any presumptive evidence in Shakespeare's career. In 1601 the Chamberlain's company were certainly at Aberdeen, under Laurence Fletcher ; and the production of *Macbeth,* early in the reign of James I, with its accurate local descriptions of Macbeth's castle and the blasted heath, certainly encourages us to think that his witches were derived from personal observation in Scotland. At Aberdeen the air would be full of men's talk about the late executions in that town for witchcraft, and of the Gowry conspiracy in 1600, whose incidents offer so close a parallel to the story of Macbeth. As the King's company only consisted of some dozen players, it is not likely that a portion was detached for this journey.

In May 1602, he again made purchases to the amount of £320; he thus acquired one hundred and seven acres of arable land in Old Stratford parish, from William Combe of Warwick, and John Combe of Old Stratford. The indenture was sealed and delivered to Gilbert Shakespeare, in his brother's absence. In September 1602, Walter Getley, by his attorney, Thomas Tibbottes, at a Court Baron of the Manor of Rowington, surrendered to him a house in Walker's Street, or Dead Lane, near New Place. At Michaelmas he bought a messuage with orchards, barns, etc., of Hercules Underhill for £60. Surely he intended to settle at Stratford.

In 1603 he was complimented in the *Microcosmos* by John Davies of Hereford. James I came to the English throne in this spring, and accepted the Chamberlain's company as his own. They are henceforth called the King's men. In 1604 Shakespeare brought an action at Stratford for £1, 5s. 10d.: he clearly had a keen eye to business.

In 1605 he bought of Ralph Hubande a thirty-one years' remainder of a lease of tithes in Stratford, Old Stratford, Bishopton, and Wilcombe, for £440. He was probably not at Stratford in this year, as he did not fill up the form for the survey of Rowington Manor on 1st August. In 1606 occurs the last marked change of style in his writing, and his fourth period begins.

In 1607 he was again complimented by John Davies in his *Scourge of Folly*. On 5th June, his daughter Susanna married Dr John Hall, a Stratford physician. But on 31st December, his youngest brother Edmund, a player, was buried at St Saviour's, Southwark.

On 16th October 1608, Shakespeare was sponsor for William Walker. On 15th March 1609, he pursued for a small debt (£6 and 24s. costs) one John Addenbrooke. In his default on 7th June he sued his surety, Thomas Hornby. J. Davies again compliments him in his *Humours Heaven on Earth*, 1609. In September 1611 he subscribed towards the costs of a bill in Parliament for amending highways. On 4th February 1612, his last surviving brother, Richard, was buried; and in 1612-13 I would date his final quittance of work. For all hope of founding a family expiring with his last male relative, and having earned amply sufficient to provide for his daughters and sister, what had he left to work for? Fame, posthumous fame, perhaps; but the man who did not print more than a quarter of his works already produced, was not likely to care deeply about that.

On 10th March 1613, he paid £80 towards the purchase of a house near Blackfriars Theatre, and mortgaged it for the £60 still unpaid. This house he let to John Robinson for ten years. In the same year, the draft of a bill in Chancery, endorsed Lane, Greene, and Shakespeare, complainants, shows that on the moiety of tithes bought by Shakespeare in 1605 too large a proportion of the reserved rent fell on the complainants. He got £120 a-year from these tithes. On 29th June the Globe Theatre, probably containing many of his MSS., was burned down, but rebuilt the same year. The fire broke out during the performance of *All is true*, Shakespeare's *Henry VIII*.

In 1614 there was a large fire in Stratford, and the corporation were busy opposing the enclosure of certain common lands. Shakespeare's name occurs on 5th September as an ancient freeholder to be compensated. On 8th October he and Thomas Greene, clerk to the corporation, covenant concerning compensation for enclosure intended by William

Replingham. Greene was sent to London, and on 17th November he writes: 'My cousin Shakespeare coming yesterday to town, I went to see how he did; and he and Mr Hall say they think there will be nothing done at all.' On 23d December, the corporation held a hall; and letters with nearly all the company's signatures were written to Mr Manyring and Mr Shakespeare, and Greene also sent his 'cousin' full particulars of the proceedings.

In 1614 we find his name in a jury list at Rowington; and in John Combe's will: but here our knowledge of him ceases, except for the last notice of all. On 25th March 1616, he made his will; on 25th April, he was buried. He died on the 23d. His daughter Judith had married Thomas Quiney, vintner, on 10th February, so that he left both his daughters settled. He just survived his last family duty. He did not long survive his public work. From poverty he had raised himself to wealth; entering on his career amid the slanders of Nash and Greene, he had lived down all sneers and sarcasms, and made himself respected; beginning work at an age (nearly thirty) when some men have exhausted themselves, he outgrew all his contemporaries; steadily pursuing his end through the travail of twenty years, he reached not only wealth, respect, and artistic power, but showed himself to be what we should judge him from his death-mask to have appeared, the nearest approach to the type of man not limited by profession, nationality, or creed, that the world has yet known. He is not only for all time, but for all places, and for all men of all times. It is not possible to tell from his writings what his birth, pursuits, politics, or creed were; and in his catholicity, no less than in his universality, we recognise his greatness, and not only worship him, but love him; because he loved all.

CHAPTER II.

WHAT POEMS AND ROMANTIC PLAYS DID SHAKESPEARE WRITE?

BEFORE proceeding to examine each of the plays of Shakespeare separately, it may be desirable to point out the method of arrangement here adopted. The common classification into comedies, histories, tragedies, separates *Pericles* and *Cymbeline* from the *Tempest* and *Winter's Tale*, thus dividing the best marked group in all the plays; again it separates *Romeo and Juliet* from the *Merchant of Venice*, and *Othello* from the other jealousy-plays. If, however, we drop this division, and adopt merely a chronological arrangement, we get the histories separated by intercalated comedies, so that a general view of them is hard to get. I propose then to divide the plays into two series—one romantic, founded on fictions, and dealing chiefly with the individual man; the other historic or rather chronicular, founded on chronicles, and dealing chiefly with man as a citizen. Our scheme will be this, the thick-typed figures marking the divisions into periods:

Romantic.	Year.	Historic.	
1. *Love's Labour's Lost.*	1592.	1 *Henry VI.*	1.
2. *Midsummer Night's Dream.*	1593.	*Richard II.*	2.
3. *Comedy of Errors.*	1594.	*Edward III.*	3.
4. *Two Gentlemen of Verona.*	1595.	*Richard III* (Q.).	4.
5. *Romeo and Juliet* (Q. 1, Q. 2).	1596.	*John.*	5.
6. *Merchant of Venice.*	1597.	1 *Henry IV.*	6.
7. *Much Ado about Nothing.*	1598.	2 *Henry IV.*	7.
8. *Merry Wives of Windsor* (Q.).	1599.	*Henry V.*	8.
9. *Taming of the Shrew.*	1599-1600.		
10. *As You Like It.*	1600.	*Julius Cæsar.*	9.
11. *Twelfth Night.*	1601.	*Hamlet* (Q. 1).	10.
12. *All's Well that Ends Well.*	1602.	*Richard III* (F.).	
13. *Measure for Measure.*	1603.	*Macbeth.*	11.
14. *Othello; Merry Wives of Windsor* (F.).	1604.	*Hamlet* (Q. 2).	
15. *Troylus and Cressida.*	1605.	*Lear.*	12.
16. *Pericles.*	1606.	*Timon.*	13.

Romantic.	Year.	Historic.	
	1607.	*Antony and Cleopatra.*	14.
	1608.	*Coriolanus.*	15.
17. *Cymbeline.*	1609.		
18. *Winter's Tale.*	1610.		
19. *Tempest.*	1611.		
	1612.	*Two Noble Kinsmen.*	16.
	1613.	*Henry VIII.*	17.

These are all the plays generally attributed to Shakespeare; there are a number of others which are called doubtful. Some of these are by no means doubtful; for they are known to be by other authors, or for companies which he never was connected with. Some, however, he may have had a hand in, if they were written for Lord Strange's company before 1594, or for the Chamberlain's or King's company after that date. There is *primâ facie* evidence rendering inquiry desirable. But this must not be confined to mere questions of taste, the history of the stage must also be considered. This has been hitherto unduly neglected.

I will first notice the writings not dramatic, to clear them out of our way.

POEMS.

Besides his plays, Shakespeare wrote poems, namely:

VENUS AND ADONIS.

This he calls 'The first heir of my invention.' It was entered 18th April 1593, was dedicated to Henry Wriothesley, Earl of Southampton, and was very popular.

Editions:* Q. 1, 1593; Q. 2, 1594; Q. 3, 1596; Q. 4, 1599; Q. 5, 1600; Q. 6, 7, 1602; Q. 8, 1617; Q. 9, 1620; Q. 10, 1627; Q. 11 (?), 1630; Q. 12, 1630; Q. 13, 1636.

THE RAPE OF LUCRECE.

This also was dedicated to the same patron. It was entered 9th May 1594.

Editions: Q. 1, 1594; Q. 2, 1598; Q. 3, 1600; Q. 4, 1607; Q. 5, 1616; Q. 6, 1624.

* Where quarto editions of plays or poems exist, they are thus noticed at the end of each article. Where there is no notice to a play, it was first published in the 1623 folio.

SONNETS.

These were in existence in 1598. It would be impossible here even to enumerate the theories that have been promulgated about them. Some have looked on them as one poem; some as several—of groups of sonnets; some as containing a separate poem in each sonnet. They have been supposed to be written in Shakespeare's own person, or in the character of another, or of several others; to be autobiographical or heterobiographical, or allegorical; to have been addressed to Lord Southampton, to Sir William Herbert, to his own wife, to Lady Rich, to his child, to his nephew, to himself, to his muse. The 'W. H.' in the dedication has been interpreted as William Herbert, William Hughes, William Hathaway, William Hart (his nephew), William Himself, and Henry Wriothesley. But nothing certain has been advanced. I believe that W. H. is William Hart, Shakespeare's brother-in-law; that the *Sonnets* were written in 1596; that the first portion (1-126) was addressed to Lord Southampton; that they are autobiographical, and constitute one poem. The remainder, I think, were addressed to Anne Shakespeare, his wife, but with a very different interpretation from that usually put on them. My interpretation, whether right or wrong, fits in singularly with what we know of Shakespeare's life from other sources. I do not find that the other interpretations I have seen fit in at all. The *Sonnets* were published in 1609, but not by Shakespeare, along with *A Lover's Complaint*.

The *Passionate Pilgrim* was published in 1599, and again in 1612. It is only partly Shakespeare's.

The *Phœnix and the Turtle* is extracted from *Love's Martyr, or Rosalin's Complaint*, by Robert Chester, 1601.

ROMANTIC PLAYS.

LOVE'S LABOUR'S LOST. *Circa* 1592.

This was almost certainly Shakespeare's earliest comedy. As we now have it, however, it is a 'corrected and newly augmented' version, as presented before Queen Elizabeth at Christmas, 1597. The pun on Ajax (V, ii, 579) is probably derived from Harrington's *Metamorphosis of Ajax*, 1596; and 'the first and second cause, passado, duello,' etc. (I, ii, 184, etc.), from Saviolo's *Treatise of Honour and Honourable*

Quarrels, 1595. These passages and the repetition in V, ii, 827-832, enable us to distinguish some of the new insertions. The origin of the play is unknown. The sonnets in it appear again in *Sonnets* 127, 137. There was a companion play called *Love's Labour's Won*.

Editions: Q. 1, 1598; Q. 2, 1631.

MIDSUMMER NIGHT'S DREAM. *c.* 1593.

The main plot, as far as we know, may be Shakespeare's own: hints for the framework may have been derived from Chaucer's *Knight's Tale*, or North's *Plutarch;* for Pyramus and Thisbe, from Chaucer's *Thisbe of Babylon*, or Golding's translation of Ovid's *Metamorphoses;* for Oberon and the fairies, from Greene's *James IV of Scotland*, and popular tales. Oberon and Titania had been introduced in a dramatic entertainment before Queen Elizabeth in 1591. *Procris and Cephalus* by H. Chettle was entered for publication in 1593. 'The thrice three muses mourning for the death of learning, late deceased in beggary,' alludes to Spenser's *Tears of the Muses*, 1591, and also, I think, to the death of Greene in 1592. The allusions to the bad weather of 1593 are very palpable (II, i, 88, etc.). This play as we have it, is a revised edition made for publication in 1600. It may have been added to, as well as revised.

Editions: Q. 1, 1600; Q. 2, 1600.

COMEDY OF ERRORS. *c.* 1594.

This play may have been founded on the *Historie of Error*, shown at Hampton Court, at New Year's Day at night, 1576-7, enacted by the Children of Paul's; and on William Warner's translation of Plautus' *Menæchmi*, 1595. Warner's play was entered at Stationers' Hall 10th June 1594; but the printer's advertisement states that it had been circulated previously in manuscript. A play called a *Comedy of Errors* (like to Plautus his *Menæchmi*), was acted at Gray's Inn in December 1594. This may have been Warner's, but was probably Shakespeare's. The pun on 'France making war against her hair' (heir), fixes a limit of date; for Henri IV, the heir of France, was warring for his succession from August 1589 to his coronation February 1594. This play we have only in its acting form, probably much abridged, as Shakespeare did not publish it in quarto.

Two Gentlemen of Verona. *c.* 1595.

A play called *Felix and Philomena*, founded on Montemayor's story of the shepherdess Filismena, was exhibited at Greenwich in 1584. The translation of the story itself, by Bartholomew Young, existed in MS. in 1583, but was not printed till 1598. Bandello's novel of *Apollonius and Sylla* was translated in 1581. On these two stories Shakespeare's play is founded. The praise of solitude (V, iv), and Valentine's scene with the robbers (IV, i), were taken from Sidney's *Arcadia*, Book I, ch. 6. 'Some to the wars to try their fortunes there' (I, iii, 8), may refer to the expected invasion by the Spaniards in 1595, when English troops were sent to aid Henri IV. 'Some to discover islands far away' (I, iii, 9), may refer to Raleigh's voyage to discover Guiana in 1595, or Sir Humphrey Gilbert's in 1594. The pestilence mentioned in II, i, 22, most probably does refer to the plague of 1593; and the allusion in I, i, 22, to *Hero and Leander*, most likely was written after the circulation in MS., 1594, of Marlow's poem, published 1598. Shakespeare frequently refers to this story; but in no other play earlier than 1596. This play, like the *Comedy of Errors*, was not published by Shakespeare, hence we have only an abridged, acting version of it. These early comedies which were not subsequently revised are naturally the weakest of all his plays.

Romeo and Juliet. 1596.

In the first version of this play we have remains of an older play here and there distinctly visible. This older play was, I think, written by G. Peele. It is not the old drama mentioned by Arthur Brooke, whose poem of the tragical history of *Romeus and Juliet* was the immediate foundation of the play we now have in both its versions. Shakespeare may have referred to Painter's translation of Boisteau's novel of *Rhomeo. and Julietta*, in his *Palace of Pleasure*. but I do not think he did. The date of production is fixed by the fact, that the acting company are called Lord Hunsdon's men on the title-page of the first quarto. They only had this title from 23d July 1596 to 5th March 1597, during the chamberlainship of William Brooke, Lord Cobham. There are allusions to the earthquake of 1580, the plague of 1593, Saviolo's *Book on Honour*, Daniel's *Rosamond*, etc., in the play. The fact of our having two versions of it is especially interesting. The earlier of these is surreptitious, cut down for acting purposes, and probably obtained from short-hand notes at the theatre; but there are in it passages and scenes clearly by another hand; and a careful comparision of the two versions gives us much information not only of the manner in which Shakespeare corrected his work, but also on the nature of the errors that arise at press, from mistakes in setting up type, arising out of inaccurately made corrections in the margin of the copy. The play is alluded to in Weever's *Epigrams*, published probably in 1596.

Editions: Q. 1, 1597; Q. 2, 1599; Q. 3, 1607 (?); Q. 4, 1609; Q. 5, 1637.

MERCHANT OF VENICE. *c.* 1597.

The chief plot comes indirectly from the *Pecorone* of Giovanni Fiorentino; fourth day, first novel, *Gianetta;* the casket story from an old translation of the *Gesta Romanorum*. But the immediate source was probably an old play mentioned by Gosson (1579), representing the greediness of worldly choosers, and the bloody minds of usurers. It was called *The Jew*, and was perhaps also the foundation of the *Venesyan Comedy*, acted at the Rose, under Henslow, by the Admiral's company in 1594. The notion that Shakespeare wrote this latter for a company he had never any connection with, is absurd. Marlow's *Jew of Malta* is another instance of a Jew being chosen as the villain of the story. *Wily Beguiled*, 1602-3, a play belonging to the Jonson and Dekker controversy, contains an imitation of V, i, 'In such a night,' etc.

Editions: Q. 1, 1600; Q. 2, 1600; Q. 3, 1637; Q. 4, 1652.

MUCH ADO ABOUT NOTHING. *c.* 1598.

The plot is derived indirectly from a novel of Belleforest's, after Bandello (1594). Ariosto in *Orlando Furioso*, Book V, Turberville in his *Geneura*, Spenser in his *Fairy Queen*, II, iv, 17, etc., have versions of the same story. But the immediate origin was probably the *Ariodante and Geneuora* acted before Elizabeth, 1582-3. There is an old German play by Jacob Ayres, *The Beautiful Phœnicia*, founded on Bandello, but containing points in common with Shakespeare, which are not found in Bandello. Hence there must have been an intermediate origin for both. The hero of Duke Henry of Brunswick's comedy, *Vincentius Ladislaus*, is what Beatrice describes Benedick as being, and actually causes his servant 'to set up his bills' (I, i, 39, etc.). Benedick

INTRODUCTION TO SHAKESPEARIAN STUDY. 23

and Beatrice correspond to Berowne and Rosaline in *Love's Labour's Lost*, and Mr Brae has shown that this play is almost certainly the same as *Love's Labour's Won*, mentioned by Meres in 1598. The Deformed mentioned in V, i, 317, III, iii, 181, is of course an allusion to Shakespeare himself. 'A vile thief these seven year' (III, iii, 133), indicates the time that he had been stealing, instead of inventing his plots. The 'mistaking words' of Dogberry, and the 'substantial watch,' are alluded to in the Induction of Jonson's *Bartholomew Fair*, 1614.
Edition: Q. 1, 1600.

MERRY WIVES OF WINDSOR. *c.* 1599.

Founded on *The Lovers of Pisa*, a tale in Tarleton's *News out of Purgatory*, 1589. It is said to have been written at Queen Elizabeth's desire, to show Falstaff in love. It was most likely written after the *Henry IV, V*, series, and must not be expected to be consistent with them. Nym's 'humours' certainly allude to Jonson's two plays, *Every Man in*, and *Every Man out of, his Humour*, 1588-9. The play must have been written after 1 and 2 *Henry IV*, as in these plays Falstaff was originally called Oldcastle, but not in this one. We have two versions of the play, one incomplete and surreptitious of the 1599 production, the other as it was revised, to be acted somewhere about the end of 1604. To this latter must be referred the alteration of 'council' into 'king' (I, i, 113), the allusion 'these knights will hack' (III, i, 79) to the two hundred and thirty-seven knights made by James in 1603; the lying of the court at Windsor (II, ii, 63), which refers to July 1603; the 'coach after coach' (II, ii, 66), for these vehicles were uncommon till 1605, as Howes tells us in his *Continuation of Stow's Chronicle;* and finally the reference to the Cotswold games 'outrun on Cotsale' (I, i, 92), for they were instituted by Robert Dover about 1603. Duke Frederick of Württemberg and Teck was a real 'German duke' (IV, iii), at the English court in 1592; but that date (advocated by some critics) is too early for this play.
Editions: Q. 1, 1602; Q. 2, 1619; Q. 3, 1630.

TAMING OF THE SHREW. 1599-1600 (Christmas).

Founded on the old play written for Pembroke's company in 1589, *The Taming of a Shrew*, for the Petruchio story; and on the *Supposes* of Gascoigne, Englished from Ariosto,

1566, for the story of Bianca, and some smaller matters, such as the names of Lucio and Petruchio. The old play is in some parts so like the later one, that they can hardly have been by a different hand. I assign it to Marlow and Shakespeare with confidence. The later play is only Shakespeare's in the Petruchio story; the Bianca part is, I think, by T. Lodge; Lodge has scarcely made any use of the old play. He uses Baptista as a man's name; Shakespeare, at this same date or a year after, in *Hamlet*, as a woman's. There is no induction to any other play of Shakespeare's. There is an allusion in the play to *Patient Grissel*. A play of this name, which, like Dekker's *Medicine for a Curst Wife*, July 1602, was certainly an opposition play to this one, was acted at the Rose in January 1600. It was written by Dekker, Chettle, and Haughton, and contains three allusions to the *Taming of the Shrew*. These mutual allusions show contemporaneity. There also appears to be an allusion to Heywood's *Woman Killed with Kindness* in the line, 'This is the way to kill a wife with kindness,' but this expression was proverbial, and if an allusion is meant, may have been a subsequent insertion. The play can hardly have been so late as March 1603, when Heywood's was produced. The exact date is, I believe, fixed by the great frost of 1599-1600. Compare Grumio's description in IV, i.

Edition : Q. 1, 1631.

As You Like It. *c.* 1600.

Founded on Lodge's novel *Rosalynd, or Euphues' Golden Legacy*, 1590. 'Stayed,' that is, forbidden to be published, along with *Henry V, Much Ado about Nothing*, and *Every Man in his Humour*, in the Stationers' books on 4th August. The year is not given, but as *Henry V* and *Much Ado about Nothing* were again entered in August 1600, on the 14th and 23d respectively, and printed accordingly, it is tolerably certain that this year was the one in question. The staying was probably carried out because the play was still acting at the Globe. Again, Stow mentions the image of Diana referred to in IV, i, 145, 'I will weep like Diana in the fountain,' as set up in 1598, and decayed in 1603. The date is therefore fixed to 1599 or 1600. A line is quoted from Marlow's *Hero and Leander* (III, v, 83), referring to him as the 'dead shepherd,' which was published in 1598. Shakespeare is said to have acted the part of Adam.

TWELFTH NIGHT. 1601.

The plot of Viola's story is derived from the story of *Apollonius and Sylla*, already noticed under the *Two Gentlemen of Verona*. I believe this part of the play was written in 1595. But the complete work was certainly produced in 1601. Manningham saw it acted at the Middle Temple on 2d February 1602. This play has also a second name, *What You Will*, which was taken by Marston for a play of his published in 1607, but written some years earlier. The name, *Twelfth Night*, was probably derived from the date of its production. It may be noticed here that as the year in Shakespeare's time ended at Easter in some reckonings, at 25th March in others, Twelfth night, 1600, would fall in 1601. Throughout this book modern dates are given where they can be ascertained; but in considerations of dates on title-pages, etc., the old reckoning must be borne in mind. Duke in this play is synonymous with Count, as it is with Emperor in the *Two Gentlemen of Verona*, and with King in *Love's Labour's Lost*. Shakespeare does not commit this mistake in plays written after 1595.

ALL'S WELL THAT ENDS WELL. c. 1602.

The main plot is founded on *Giletta of Narbonne*, in Painter's *Palace of Pleasure*, Vol. I. This play, like all the others between 1600 and 1602, is a revised and augmented version of an older one of Shakespeare's. It is not, however, as shown by Mr Brae, a later version of *Love's Labour's Won*. The present title is alluded to in several places in the play itself, which are clearly part of the early work. The underplot (comic part with Parolles) is, as usual with Shakespeare, of his own invention. In plays that he re-wrote the underplot is generally the new portion. There are resemblances pointed out by Elze between this play and *Hamlet* that confirm the date here given to it. It is likely that the journey to Scotland in 1601, and the not having to act at Court in that year, obviated the necessity of producing new plays at this time.

MEASURE FOR MEASURE. 1603.

Founded on Whetstone's *Promos and Cassandra*, in his *Heptameron of Civil Discourses*, 1582. Its date is fixed as soon after James's accession, by the following allusions to facts:

> ' I'll privily away. I love the people,
> But do not like to stage me to their eyes.
> Though it [? I] do well, I do not relish well
> Their loud applause and aves vehement '—I, i.

> ' The general, subject to a well-wisht king,
> Quit their own part, and in obsequious fondness
> Crowd to his presence, where their untaught love
> Must needs appear offense '—II, iv.

This apologises for James's ungracious entry into England. It had been proclaimed that the people should not resort to him.

> ' What with the war, what with the sweat, . . .
> Heaven grant us peace '—I, ii.

The war with Spain was ended on the 19th August 1604; but James had shown his peaceful intentions in 1603. There was a plague in 1603. In London 30,000 died of it. The list of prisoners in IV, iii, contains four stabbers. The roaring boys, bravados, roysters, etc., were so numerous in 1603, that the statute of stabbing was passed in the early part of 1604.

OTHELLO. c. 1604.

Founded on a novel of Giraldi Cinthio, in the *Hecatomithi*, Dec. iii, Nov. 3. The names of Othello and Iago occur in Reynolds' *God's Revenge against Adultery*. There is an historical foundation for part of the plot. In May 1570, Mustapha, the general of Solyman II, attacked Cyprus. The Turkish fleet first sailed towards Cyprus, then went to Rhodes, met another squadron, and resumed its course for Rhodes, which was taken in 1571. The relation concerning cannibals and 'men whose heads do grow beneath their shoulders,' is taken from Raleigh's narrative of the *Discovery of Guiana*, 1600. He was resolved of their truth. In this play we find a clown for the last time in Shakespeare. There has been one in every comedy since 1599 that was entirely written by him.

Dekker's *Patient Man*, I, i (1604):

> ' Thou kill'st her now again,
> And art more savage than a barbarous Moor,'

alludes to *Othello*. So does probably *Ram Alley* about the same date:

> ' Villain, slave ! thou hast wronged my wife;'

and Malone, who never wrote at random, says that he knew that the play was acted in 1604; hence I ascribe it to that year.

Editions: Q. 1, 1622; Q. 2, 1630.

TROYLUS AND CRESSIDA. c. 1605.

Founded on Chaucer's *Troilus and Cresseide* for the love story, and on Caxton's *Troy Book* for the war story. Thersites is taken from Chapman's *Homer, Iliad*, i-vii, 1597 This play was originally acted by the Chamberlain's men c. 1601, and was so entered for publication 7th February 1603. The idea that Dekker and Chettle's play of 1599, acted by the Admiral's men at the Rose, could have been so entered, needs no confutation. The play was re-written (except the love story which remains nearly unchanged) before 1606, the latest date assignable to *Pericles* and the beginning of Shakespeare's fourth manner, and was printed in 1609, piratically, as a play 'not staled with the stage.' It was first acted in its present form in 1609. It is always placed with the tragedies. Its proper place is with the comedies. It is so called in the prologue. Its production in the earlier form is proved by a passage in *Histriomastix*, which was written before Elizabeth's death.

> ' *Troy*. Come, Cressida, my cresset light,
> Thy face doth shine both day and night.
> Behold, behold *thy garter blue*,
> *Thy knight his valiant elbow wears.*
> That when he SHAKES his furious SPEARE,
> The foe, in shivering fearful sort,
> May lay him down in death to snort.
> *Cress.* O knight, with valour in thy face,
> Here take my screene, wear it for grace ;
> Within thy helmet put the same,
> Therewith to make thy enemies lame.'

Much of the fifth act has been suspected to be spurious. It may be only early.

Edition: Q. 1 (*bis*), 1609.

PERICLES. 1606.

Shakespeare wrote only the Marina story in this play. The first three acts were written by Wilkins; the prose parts, and the long-lined choruses probably by Rowley. The play is founded on T. Twine's *Painful Adventures of Prince Appolonius*, etc., entered in 1576, republished in 1607. Gower's version of the same story in his *Confessio Amantis* is sometimes preferred. The play was entered by Blount, 2d May 1608, but published by Gosson. This play, like *Love's Labour's Lost*, seems to have been used by Shakespeare as a repertory of hints for after-works for several years. Even the lapse of time between the acts of fifteen years is repeated in *Winter's Tale*.

Act III, sc. ii, is palpably imitated in the *Puritan*, IV, iii, published 1607. But this play was acted in 1606, as a Sunday on the 13th July is mentioned in it, which was the case in 1600, 1606, 1612; and the only one of these dates admissible is 1606. Tyrwhitt (quoted by Sir W. Scott!) has confused the old and new styles, and assigned wrong years to this coincidence. *Pericles* cannot therefore be later than 1606.

Editions: Q. 1, Q. 2, 1609; Q. 3, 1611; Q. 4, 1619; Q. 5, 1630; Q. 6, 1635.

CYMBELINE. *c.* 1609.

Founded on Holinshed's *Chronicles*. The story of Hay and his sons staying his countrymen in a lane during a battle, is in the Scotland portion of that writer. The reign of Cymbeline is of course given in his England. The story of Iachimo is found in Boccaccio, Day 11, Novel 9. The adventures in the wilderness occur in the fairy tale of *Schneewitchen:* but whence Shakespeare got them we do not know. The character of Imogen is distinctly imitated in Beaumont's *Philaster*, which cannot date later than 1611 (Dyce puts it in 1608). Dr S. Forman, the astrological quack, saw the play acted in 1610 or 1611. The vision in IV, iv, has been generally considered to be an insertion by an inferior hand.

WINTER'S TALE. 1610.

Founded on Greene's *Dorastus and Fawnia*, or, as it was at first called, *Pandosto, or The Triumph of Time*, 1588. Dr Simon Forman saw the play performed 15th May 1611, and Sir Henry Herbert in his *Office Book* mentions it as an old play, allowed by Sir G. Buck. But Buck was made Master of the Revels in August 1610. Hence our limits of date. Jonson in his *Bartholomew Fair* (Induction, 1614) says: 'If there be never a *servant-monster* in the Fair who can help it, nor a *nest of antics*. He is loath to make Nature afraid in his plays, like those that beget *Tales, Tempests*, and such like drolleries.' The servant-monster is Caliban. The nest of antics are the satyrs (IV, iv, 352) in our present play. Jonson had, in 1614, left the Chamberlain's company for the Lady Elizabeth's. Hence these sneers at the Globe plays. In his conversations with Drummond of Hawthornden, he said that Shakespeare wanted art and sometimes sense, for in one of his plays he brought in a number of men saying they had suffered shipwreck in Bohemia, where is no sea near by 100 miles.

TEMPEST. 1611.

Founded on the following narratives: 1. A pamphlet describing the tempest that dispersed the fleet of Sir George Somers and Sir Thomas Gates, when the admiral-ship was wrecked on the island of Bermuda (December 1609, January 1610). 2. Jourdan's narrative, in which the Bermudas is called the Isle of Devils (13th October 1610). 3. *The True Declaration of the Council of Virginia* (1610). 4. A true repertory of the wreck and redemption of Sir Thomas Gates, knight, upon and from the Islands of the Bermudas, by William Strachey. Gonzalo's description of his ideal republic (II, i) is from Florio's *Montaigne*, 1603. This play as we have it, is a copy abridged for acting purposes. One character, Duke of Milan's son (I, ii, 438), has been entirely struck out; unless Francisco is the same character, or rather the remainder of it. It is noticeable that Stephăno occurs in this play; Stephāno in *Merchant of Venice*, 1597. Shakespeare acted in Jonson's *Every Man in his Humour*, in 1598. Stephăno is a character in that play.

CHAPTER III.

WHAT HISTORIES OR CHRONICLE PLAYS DID SHAKESPEARE WRITE?

1 Henry VI.

THIS play is founded on Holinshed, but does not follow him so closely as the histories that are undoubtedly written by Shakespeare. It is certainly the play produced at the Rose by Lord Strange's players, on 3d March 1592. It was consequently always in the possession of the company to which Shakespeare belonged. It is referred to in the epilogue to *Henry V.* The greater part of it is certainly not Shakespeare's; the part containing the episode of Talbot's son (IV, ii, vii; V, ii) is evidently an insertion, and was probably written in 1592, by Shakespeare. The early part of the play (I, i, to III, iii) was, I think, written by Peele (I, iii; III, i) and Marlow (all the other scenes); II, iv, v, being probably of much later date, and inserted by Shakespeare. In the latter part of the play, IV, ii-vii, and (?) V, ii, are, in my opinion (confirmed by Mr Swinburne's), by Shakespeare; V, i, iii$b$ (l. 45 to end), iv$b$ (l. 33 to end), by Peele; while III, iv, IV, i, V, iii$a$, iv$a$, v, seem to be Marlow altered, possibly by Lodge or Nash. The versification is very like the *Dido*, which was written by Marlow, and revised by Nash. The division of this play given in my article on *Henry VI* in *Macmillan's Magazine*, and thoughtlessly copied into my *Shakespeare Manual*, was printed from a slip prepared for a different purpose, through a mistake of mine. It is, of course, quite wrong. The play is called the third part of *Henry VI* in Blount and Jaggard's entry in the Stationers' books, in 1623. Hence it was written after 2 *Henry VI*, and 3 *Henry VI*, which are called the first and second parts in the assignment made from Pavier to Millington, 19th April 1602. Nash in his *Piers Penniless' Supplication*, 1592, thus writes of a play, surely this one: 'How would it have joyed brave Talbot, the terror

of the French, to think that after he had lain two hundred
years in his tomb, he should triumph again on the stage, and
have his bones new embalmed with the tears of ten thousand
spectators at least (at several times), who, in the tragedian
that represents his person, imagine they behold him fresh
bleeding.'

RICHARD II. *c.* 1593-4.

This play is founded on Holinshed's *Chronicle*. It is
singularly like Marlow's *Edward II* in many points, and it
is not improbable that Marlow began it, and that Shakespeare used his unfinished sketch in making his own drama.
It dates *c.* 1593-4. A play, called *Henry IV* in the state
trials, in which Richard II was deposed and killed on the
stage, was performed at a public theatre (Globe), at the request of Sir Gilly Merrick and other followers of Essex, on
the afternoon before his insurrection in 1601. Augustine
Phillips, who managed the Globe company, had forty shillings extra to play it, as the play was old, and would not
draw. Camden calls it ' *exoleta tragedia de tragica abdicatione Richardi II.*' The abdication scene (IV, i) had previously been suppressed, and was not indeed printed till 1608.
Except on this occasion it was probably not acted after 1596,
the year in which the pope issued a bull exhorting rebellion
against Elizabeth.' In 1599 Hayward was censured in the
Star Chamber and imprisoned, for publishing his *History of
the First Year of Henry IV*, which is simply the story of the
deposition of Richard II. Forman in his *Diary* mentions a
play of *Richard II;* but this was *The Life and Death of
Jack Straw*, published in 1593, revived in 1610-11.

Editions: Q. 1, 1597; Q. 2, 1598; Q. 3, 1608; Q. 4, 1615;
Q. 5, 1634.

EDWARD III. 1594.

Probably written in 1594. It was published in 1596, as
having been played sundry times about the city of London.
The theatres were shut on account of the plague in 1593, and
the Chamberlain's company played at Newington Butts, the
Crosskeys, and other places, in 1594 and 1595. It is founded
for the historical part on Holinshed, but contains an episode
of the attempt at seduction of the Countess of Salisbury by
Edward III, in I, ii, II. This part is probably Shakespeare's;
the rest Peele's. Whether the whole was revised by Shakespeare is doubtful, but very likely. Mr Tennyson tells me
he can trace the master's hand all through the play. It

contains a line afterwards introduced by Shakespeare in *Sonnet* 94:

> 'Lilies that fester smell far worse than weeds.'

The following passage seems to fix the date:

> ' Arise, true English lady! whom our isle
> May better boast of than e'er Roman might
> Of her whose ransackt treasury hath taskt
> The vain endeavours of so many pens'—II, ii.

This allusion to Lucrece must surely be taken in conjunction with the fact that Shakespeare's *Rape of Lucrece* was published in 1594. Heywood's play also belongs to the same year, in my opinion.

Editions: Q. 1, 1596; Q. 2, 1599; Q. 3, 1609; Q. 4, 1617; Q. 5, 1625.

RICHARD III.

This play was founded on Holinshed, with a few hints from a preceding play produced by the Queen's company, published in 1594. It is alluded to in Weever's *Epigrams*, which also mention *Romeo*, and therefore cannot be dated earlier than 1596. It is most likely that it was begun by Peele, and finished and revised by Shakespeare, as we have it in the first quarto, published 1597. The second version as we have it in the folio, was certainly corrected on a copy of the 1602 quarto; most likely in that year, as then Jonson, who had not yet returned to the Globe after leaving it in 1599, was writing his *Richard Crookback* for the Admiral's company. The nature and extent of the differences between the quarto and folio texts are unparalleled in any other play; and the alterations are such as to make it less like Peele and more like Shakespeare. The play stands between 2, 3 *Henry VI* (which the external evidence shows that Shakespeare did not write, even if he corrected them), and Shakespeare's other historical plays.

Editions: Q. 1, 1597; Q. 2, 1598; Q. 3, 1602; Q. 4, 1605; Q. 5, 1612; Q. 6, 1622; Q. 7, 1629; Q. 8, 1634.

JOHN.

This play is founded on the *Troublesome Reign of John, King of England*, published in 1591. It follows the plot, and borrows many ideas, and one line; but is far more Shakespearian than the preceding historical plays. He here begins to work with entire freedom. The date is almost certainly 1596.

> 'A braver choice of dauntless spirits,
> Than now the English bottoms have waft' o'er,
> Did never float upon the swelling tide,
> To do offence and scathe to Christendom'—II, i.

This surely alludes to the great fleet sent against Spain in 1596. It sailed on 3d June, destroyed their armada, sacked Cadiz, and returned on 8th August. Hamnet Shakespeare died on August 12th. Constance's lament for Arthur's loss seems to show Shakespeare's feelings on this matter. This is the first history properly so called. *Richard II* and *Richard III* are called tragedies in their titles, and rightly so.

1 Henry IV. 1597.

This play was founded on Holinshed's *Chronicles*, and a preceding play of 7th May 1592, *The Famous Victories of Henry V.* It must be dated 1597. It was entered for publication 25th February 1598. Shakespeare has followed Holinshed, even in confounding the two Mortimers into one. In this play he first introduces prose as an essential element in his histories, and reaches his highest point in comedy in the character of Falstaff.

Editions: Q. 1, 1598; Q. 2, 1599; Q. 3, 1604; Q. 4, 1608; Q. 5, 1613; Q. 6, 1622; Q. 7, 1632; Q. 8, 1639.

2 Henry IV. 1597-8.

Founded on the same as the preceding. 'Must be dated before 25th February 1598,' say the critics, because there is in the quarto *Old.* for *Oldcastle*, prefixed to one of the speeches; whereas the entry of 1 *Henry IV* mentions Sir John Falstaff. Hence the change of Oldcastle into Falstaff must have been made after the writing of the second play, and before the date of entry. I think it more likely that a writer who had written *Old.* some hundreds of times in 1 *Henry IV*, should by a slip put it for *Fal.* in the second, than that a corrector, looking for this name, and this only, should omit to correct it. A more powerful argument is, that in III, ii, Falstaff speaks of having been page to Thomas Mowbray, Duke of Norfolk. Oldcastle did hold that position. Justice Shallow is alluded to in *Every Man in his Humour*, 1598. The name Oldcastle was taken from *The Famous Victories of Henry V.*

C

Falstaff is alluded to under the name of Oldcastle in several works in 1604. It is clear that when Shakespeare first adopted this name, he did not know that this was the Lollard martyr, Lord Cobham. The play of *Sir John Oldcastle*, 1599, refers to Shakespeare, as the Admiral's company's poets might be expected to do:

> 'It is no pampered glutton *we* present,
> Nor aged counsellor to youthful sin;
> But one whose virtue shone above the rest,
> A valiant martyr and a virtuous peer.'

Edition: Q. 1, 1600.

HENRY V. 1599.

Founded on the same as the preceding. Written while the Earl of Essex was in Ireland (*see* Act V, Chorus) between April and September 1599, as promised in the epilogue of 2 *Henry IV*, which must therefore be placed as near this play as possible, that is, in 1598. We have two versions of this play, as of *Romeo and Juliet*, and the *Merry Wives of Windsor*. In this instance, however, the first version is not a first sketch, but merely a copy taken down in shorthand at the theatre, and published by the piratical printer, Thomas Pavier. The reference to 'this wooden O' in the prologue, fixes the date as not earlier than 1599, when the Globe was built.

Editions: Q. 1, 1600; Q. 2, 1602; Q. 3, 1608.

JULIUS CÆSAR. *c.* 1600.

Founded on North's translation of *Plutarch's Lives* of Julius Cæsar, Marcus Brutus, and Marcus Antonius. Mr Halliwell has found an allusion to it dating 1601, and the style and metre are too like the preceding histories to allow us to place it later. An opposition play called *Cæsar's Fall*, was acted in May 1602 by the Admiral's company. Shakespeare's play was revived (in an altered form?) in 1613, with the title, *Cæsar's Tragedy*. As Shakespeare had then probably retired from the stage, and our present copy* is clearly an abridged one made for acting purposes, it was most likely abridged by another hand. From the spelling Antonie (Shakespeare in other plays spells Anthonie without exception), the alteration of 'Cæsar doth never wrong but with just cause,' and certain similarities of phrase with Jonson's writings, I think his is the most likely hand to have abridged it.

* It is called *Life and Death of Julius Cæsar* in Catalogue of F. 1.

HAMLET. *c.* 1601.

Founded on an old play now lost, acted by the players of Lord Pembroke in 1589, and on the *History of Hamlet* (black-letter), taken from one of Belleforest's novels Shakespeare may have had a hand in the old play. The reference to the inhibition of the players (II, ii, 346) may apply to the first order of the Privy Council to restrain the immoderate use of playhouses, 22d June 1600, but more likely to their second order, 31st December 1601, when Shakespeare had just returned from Scotland. The Globe and Fortune were allowed to remain open; the other theatres were closed on account of the personal satire they had indulged in. Nash's allusion to 'whole Hamlets, I should say handfuls, of tragical speeches,' 1589, fixes the date of the old play; Lodge also alludes to the Ghost which cried so miserably at the theatre like an oyster wife, 'Hamlet, revenge!' (*Wit's Misery*, 1596). The play was entered 26th July 1602. It was probably acted in 1601-2. The surreptitious first quarto seems to be made up of Shakespeare's first draft and the old 1589 play. But the names Corambis and the like must belong to Shakespeare's first copy, and cannot be alterations of the printers. The second quarto is the result of a revision made in 1604. It alludes to the Revels Children, then recently set up at Blackfriars (January 1604). The folio version is still further altered for stage purposes by insertions and omissions; but is on the whole the best and most authentic; as in all plays from this date onward.

Editions: Q. 1, 1603; Q. 2, 1604; Q. 3, 1605; Q. 4, 1607? Q. 5, 1611; Q. 6, 1637.

MACBETH. *c.* 1603.

Founded on Holinshed's *Chronicle*, and Reginald Scott's *Discovery of Witchcraft*, 1584; also on an earlier play. Kempe in his *Nine Days' Wonders Performed in a Dance from London to Norwich* (April 1600), refers to a ballad (play) whose author was found at the Bankside (Globe), sitting at a play: 'A proper upright youth, only for a little stooping in the shoulders, all Hart to the heel, a penny poet' (writer for a public theatre like the Globe, where the lowest charge for entrance was a penny), 'whose first making was the miserable stolen story of *Mac-do-el*, or *Mac-do-beth*, or *Mac* somewhat, for I am sure a *Mac*' (pronounce *Mauk*) 'it was, though I had never the maw to see it.' He advises the author to 'leave writing these beastly ballads; make not good wenches prophetesses for little or no profit.' This 'ballad' was entered at Stationers' Hall 27th August 1596. I see no reason to doubt that it was the earliest attempt of Shakespeare in tragedy, made in 1589, and that he is the penny poet alluded to. For Kempe left the Globe for the Earl of Worcester's company when the Fortune was opened in 1600, and would naturally satirise the Globe poet. It is noticeable that Shakespeare first introduces a clown in his comedies in 1600, as if to make up for the loss of Kempe's *extempore* jigs. The other allusions accord with Shakespeare's circumstances; an 'upright man' is a sturdy beggar and thief, *i.e.* here, a plagiarist; 'stooping in the shoulders' agrees with his name Deformed. 'All Hart' may allude to the marriage of William Hart and Joan Shakespeare in 1599, probably in London, and the cordial reception of them by Shakespeare. Hart was very probably the W. H. of the *Sonnets*, mentioned in their dedication as their only begetter or collector. (How is it no one has suggested this? Every other name in W. H. or H. W. has been tried.) This being the case, and Shakespeare being in Scotland in 1601, he would naturally be interested in the Gowry conspiracy of 1600, and the witch executions then so rife. On James I acceding to the throne, Shakespeare, knowing his witch-hating character, would re-write his old play. It has in it several compliments to James: his descent from Banquo, his touching for the evil, the double balls and treble sceptres, etc. If this be so, we see why the play abounds in rhymes derived, in part, from the old play. In 1605 James was addressed at Oxford by three students of St John's College in Latin verses founded on the weird sisters' predictions. *Macbeth*, when acted at the Globe, 20th April 1610, as seen by Forman, appears not to have had the witch parts in I, i, I, iii, 1-37, nor, indeed, the scene I, ii, with the bleeding soldier. That these early witch parts, as well as all Hecate's, are spurious, there can be little doubt, after the demonstration of Messrs Clark and Wright. They were, however, wrong (and I doubly so) in rejecting various rhyming tags in the play. The weird sisters of the first act are certainly distinct from the wizards or hags of the fourth, as Holinshed makes them. In the apparently exceptional passages in III, iv, 133, IV, i, 136, the second folio reads 'wizard sisters,' not 'weird sisters.' This cannot have been an unauthorised change. Hecate was certainly inserted by Middleton after he wrote his *Witch*, from which the two 'songs' are taken. He did not write the *Witch* till 1615-6, as he was not till then a poet of the King's company. The insertion of songs went on after Middleton's time; others by an unknown hand were first inserted; then Davenant put in more of the same stamp. Had not the folio been published, and had only this later form reached us, no doubt we should have been told that these songs too were Shakespeare's. Note that 5th August 1603 was appointed for a special thanksgiving for King James's escape from the Earl of Gowry, 5th August 1600. I would date this tragedy about the same time.

LEAR. 1605-6.

Founded on Holinshed's *Chronicles*, and the old play of *The True Chronicle History of King Leir*, etc., entered 1594. The story of Gloster and his sons is taken from Sir Philip Sidney's *Arcadia;* the friends' names in III, iv, from Harsnet's *Declaration of Egregious Popish Impostures*, 1603. This play was entered in 1607 as having been played at Christmas 1606; but it was most likely played in 1605, as the old *Leir* was entered on 8th May 1605, and printed 'as lately acted' in order to deceive the public. On the other hand, it must have been after 24th October 1604, when James was proclaimed King of Great Britain, as the old line, 'I smell the blood of an *English* man' (so given by Nash, 1596), is altered into *British*. Again, 'These late eclipses of the sun and moon' (I, ii, 96); and, 'O these eclipses portend these divisions' (I, ii, 120); and, 'I am thinking, brother, of a prediction I read this other day, what should follow these eclipses' (I, ii, 124), must certainly refer to the eclipse of 2d October 1605, when the sun should be obscured eleven digits, and darkness should appear at mid-day. This eclipse was preceded by an eclipse of the moon at her 'last full.' The date may fairly be placed at Christmas 1605. The eclipses were predicted by John Harvey of King's Lynn, in his *Discoursive Problem concerning Prophesies*, 1588.
Editions: Q. 1, Q. 2, 1608.

TIMON OF ATHENS. 1606.

Founded on a passage in Plutarch's *Life of Antonius*, and the twenty-eighth novel of Painter's *Palace of Pleasure;* partly also on the old play of *Timon* of 1603 (?), and, in the part not Shakespeare's, on Lucian's *Dialogues*. Shakespeare's share is I, i (verse part); II, i, ii (verse part); III, vi (verse part); IV, i, iii, 1-291, 363-398, 414-453; V, i (verse part), ii, iv. Cyril Tourneur was the only person connected with the King's company at this time who could have written the other part. Wilkins is out of the question. There can be no doubt of the date. It must lie between *Lear* and the later Roman plays, from metrical and internal evidence.

ANTHONY AND CLEOPATRA. 1607.

Founded on Plutarch's *Life of Marcus Antonius*. Entered for publication 20th May 1608, and, no doubt, written in the preceding year.

CORIOLANUS. *c.* 1608.

Founded on Plutarch's *Life of Coriolanus*. Menenius' fable, however, is from Camden's *Remains*, 1605. In all editions of North up to 1603, in the passage corresponding to V, i, 98, 'unfortunately' is printed for 'unfortunate;' after Shakespeare's correction in the play, the editions of North are corrected too.

THE TWO NOBLE KINSMEN. *c.* 1612.

Founded on Chaucer's *Knight's Tale*. Written by Shakespeare *c.* 1612, and subsequently altered by Fletcher. See under the next play. Shakespeare wrote of the present play, I; II, i (prose part); III, i, ii; IV, iii; V, i, iii, iv.
Edition: Q. 1, 1634.

HENRY VIII. 1613.

Founded on Holinshed's *Chronicle*, and Fox's *Christian Martyrs*, 1563. The play as we have it is an alteration made subsequently by Fletcher. Shakespeare's share is I, i, ii; II, iii, iv; III, ii, 1-193; V, i. It was produced 29th June 1613. Thomas Lorkin and Sir Henry Wotton tell us this in their letters. The piece was then called *All is true*. In 1613 many names of Shakespeare's plays were changed. 1 *Henry IV* was called *Hotspur; Merry Wives of Windsor, Sir John Falstaff; Much Ado about Nothing, Benedick and Beatrice; Julius Cæsar, Cæsar's Tragedy*. I am not aware that this happened at any other date. Fletcher and Shakespeare certainly did not work together on either this or the preceding play. The 'making new nations' (V, v, 51), alludes to the colonising Virginia, for which there was a state lottery in 1612.

W. Rowley's play, *When you see me you know me* (on Henry VIII), and the drama of *Lord Cromwell*, were reprinted in 1613, with the usual fraudulent intentions. The play being called a new one in 1613, is no evidence that it was not an old one altered. Such pieces were always called new. But from 1611 to 1614, Fletcher was writing for the company of the Revels Children and others, and had no traceable connection with the King's company. Hence it is almost certain that the versions of this and the preceding play produced by him were of later date than 1614. The original copies were probably partially destroyed in the fire at the Globe. The present prologue and epilogue must have been written for the play as revised with Fletcher's alteration, for two reasons: *Firstly*, they contain the rhymes, *See, story, In, women*, which are not in Shakespeare's late manner; *secondly*, 'a shilling' is mentioned as the price of seats, which applies not to the Globe, but to Blackfriars. The critics quote this line, as showing that the prices at this public theatre were the same as at a private one, in the teeth of all evidence to the contrary. Another play, *The History of Cardenio*, was acted at court in 1613, and entered as Shakespeare and Fletcher's in 1653; but this has been identified with the *Double Falsehood*, published in an altered form by Theobald, and attributed by Dyce to Shirley, who thus assumes the existence of two plays of this title.

In the above notices several plays, viz., *The Taming of the Shrew* (?), *Timon, Macbeth, Julius Cæsar, The Two Noble Kinsmen*, and *Henry VIII*, are spoken of as having been altered from Shakespeare's original copies. I cannot give here the enormous mass of evidence which I have gathered as to the prevalence of this practice, and the unlikelihood of Shakespeare's plays being an exception to it. But as the date of these alterations is of some interest, I may note that from 1616 to 1623, Fletcher, Jonson, Middleton, and probably Tourneur and Lodge, were the only poets of the King's company. As it is precisely to these writers that I have attributed the alterations on other grounds, I further suggest that the date of them must belong to this period, except, perhaps, *The Taming of the Shrew*, the MSS. having been damaged, as already suggested, in the fire at the Globe. We find no trace of such refashioning by second hands in the plays published in quarto, but merely a few comparatively slight omissions, insertions, etc., for acting purposes.

CHAPTER IV.

WHAT OTHER PLAYS HAVE BEEN ASCRIBED TO SHAKESPEARE?

BESIDES the plays in the preceding chapters, others have been ascribed to Shakespeare, of which the following list contains the names of all with which he can, by any possibility, have had to do in any way:

2 *Henry VI*,	*c*. 1591	All belonged to Pembroke's company, and afterwards to Chamberlain's.
3 *Henry VI*,	*c*. 1592	
Titus Andronicus,	1594	
Fair Emm,	1590	All belonged to L. Strange's company.
London Prodigal,	1591	
Arden of Feversham,	*c*. 1592	
Locrine,	1595	Edited by W. S.
Mucedorus,	published 1598	All belonged to Chamberlain's company.
Cromwell,	,, 1602	
'Larum for London,	,, 1602	
Warning for Fair Women,	,, 1602	
Yorkshire Tragedy,	,, 1608	Belonged to King's company.
Merry Devil of Edmonton,	,, 1608	
Birth of Merlin,	,, 1662	Published as Rowley's and Shakespeare's.

Other plays have been ascribed to him, which he cannot have touched, unless he belonged to the Queen's company before 1589, namely:

Troublesome Reign of King John (Queen's company).
Sir John Oldcastle (Admiral's).
Puritan (Children of Paul's).
King Leir (Queen's).
Richard III (Queen's) (the 1594 play).

I append notices of such of these as the reader is likely to meet with.

2 AND 3 HENRY VI.

These plays were founded on Halle's *Chronicles*, not Holinshed's; but carelessly and regardless of historical

INTRODUCTION TO SHAKESPEARIAN STUDY. 41

blunders. They were certainly written before 1592, when Greene made his celebrated allusion to

' His tiger's heart, wrapt in a player's hide.'

Compare 3 *Henry VI*, I, iv, 137. They were most likely written by Peele and Marlow, Marlow's share being 2 *Henry VI*, I, iii*b*, III, ii, iii, IV, i; and 3 *Henry VI*, II, V. The quarto editions are clearly shorthand versions, taken down at the theatre piratically, and not first sketches. The classical allusions and similes are in one style, both in them and in the parts added in the folio. The plays were written for Pembroke's company, and are not noticed as belonging to the King's till 1619. Probably the Chamberlain's company acquired them about 1600. The general body of critics do not agree in the view that Peele and Marlow were the original writers of these plays. Nearly all believe the portions which they assume to have been *added* in the folio version (although in the parallel cases of *Hamlet*, *Romeo and Juliet*, and *Henry V*, most of them believe the shorter versions to have been abridged for the longer), to be entirely Shakespeare's. Beyond this there is no agreement among them. Some hold the quarto versions to have been written by Shakespeare; some by Greene, Marlow, or Peele; some by Shakespeare and Greene, Marlow, or Peele. No consistent view has been evolved by any critic holding the parts in the folio which are not in the quartos to be Shakespeare's.

Editions of the pirated copies: 2 *Henry VI*, 1594, 1600, 1619; 3 *Henry VI*, 1595, 1600, 1619.

TITUS ANDRONICUS. 1594.

This play was produced 23d January 1594, by the Admiral's or the Chamberlain's company. It was then a new play. It was before 1600 played successively by the companies of Sussex, Pembroke, and Darby; and was probably written by George Peele. It was in the possession of the Chamberlain's company in 1600, probably not before, as they are not mentioned in p. 1 of Q. 1. But there was another play on this subject, of which Shakespeare probably was the author. It was called *Titus and Vespasian*, and was acted 11th April 1592, at the Rose, by Lord Strange's men. A version of this play will be found in Cohn's *Shakespeare in Germany*. This is probably the play which Jonson refers to as dating twenty-five years back in 1614, which brings it to 1589, the exact

date at which I believe Shakespeare began to write. He probably corrected the other play about 1600.
Editions: 1600, 1611.

FAIR EMM. 1590.

That Greene took offence at this play in 1591, is certain; that he attributed it to Shakespeare is probable, as he does not seem to have subsequently attacked any other dramatist with regard to the play; which is certainly by the same hand as the *London Prodigal*. What share Shakespeare or Lodge may have had in it is doubtful, but it must have belonged to the company of Lord Strange. That the plot is allegorical and veils Greene's own adventures, is an opinion which few share with me, but I have no doubt on the matter. William the Conqueror in this play cannot be the king of that name.
Editions: Q. 1, 1631, for John Wright; Q. 2, no date.

THE LONDON PRODIGAL. 1591.

That this play is founded on the adventures of Robert Greene, the dramatist, there can be little doubt. It also probably allegorises his connections with the various theatres then open. It was produced by Shakespeare's company, and it is certainly by the same hand as *Fair Emm*. In considering these early plays, one point seems to have escaped the critics. Before 1594 we find that each company had one poet attached to it, and only received occasional help from any others. It is not till the Admiral's company go to the Rose, in 1594, that we find more than this. In 1597 Henslow has twelve poets attached to his company; but at no period had the Chamberlain's company anything near such a number. If then Shakespeare did not write these plays, he may, if he was the then recognised poet of the company, have revised them. If he did not, T. Lodge is the only other known poet that we can connect with Lord Strange's company at this period; and he, in my opinion, wrote both this play and the preceding. The title-page has Shakespeare's name in full, as author.
Edition : 1605, T. C[reede], for N. Butter. F. 1, F. 2.

ARDEN OF FEVERSHAM. *Before* 1592.

Probably founded on an old play called *Murderous Michael*, 1578, and on Holinshed's narrative of the *Murder of Arden*, in the reign of Edward VI. It belongs to the class of domestic tragedy. The play belonged to Lord Strange's company, and was acted before 1592, when it was printed. It is not impossible that Shakespeare may have corrected this play. He is the only poet connected with Lord Strange's company that we then are sure of; and they were reduced to acting the plays of other companies in 1592, as is clear from Henslow's list.

Editions: Q. 1, 1592, for E. White; Q. 2, 1599, by J. Roberts; Q. 3, 1633, for Eliz. Allde.

LOCRINE. 1586-7.

Founded on Holinshed. Certainly, in my opinion, by the same author as *Titus Andronicus* and 3 *Henry VI*, III, ii. The comic parts are like 2 *Henry VI;* the classic quotations are like Peele. The play was probably written by Charles Tilney and Peele in 1586-7. It was republished in 1595, as 'newly set forth, overseen, and corrected by W. S.,' by T. Creede, the same printer that printed *Richard III* and *Romeo and Juliet*, the two plays, which, in my belief, were begun by Peele. In any case there is no reason whatever for doubting that the W. S. was William Shakespeare, and that he did not write, but did edit this play for his friend Peele.

Edition: Q. 1, 1595, by T. Creede. F. 1, F. 2.

MUCEDORUS. *Before* 1598.

Certainly not Shakespeare's, though a play of the King's company. It was probably written by T. Lodge, whose pastoral name Musidore was palpably taken from it with an alteration in the spelling, to introduce an allusion to his anagrammatised *nom de plume*, Golde (Musidor = Muse d'or). It was republished with additions in 1610. The additions consist of a prologue with conversations, between Comedy and Envy, at the opening and close of the piece, and two new scenes, with two new characters, Anselmo and the King of Valentia. These additions are clearly by the same hand as the original play, introduced for the performance before the king at Whitehall, Shrove Tuesday, 1610.

Editions: Q. 1, 1598, for William Jones; Q. 2, 1606 (?); Q. 3, 1609 (Collier); Q. 4, 1610; Q. 5, 1613; Q. 6, 1615, N. O[kes], for William Jones; Q. 7, 1619; Q. 8, 1621; Q. 9, 1626; Q. 10, 1634; Q. 11, 1639, for John Wright; Q. 12 (?), 1640; Q. 13, 1663, for Francis Coles; Q. 14, 1668; Q. 15 (?), 1688.

THE LIFE AND DEATH OF THOMAS LORD CROMWELL.
Before 1602.

Founded on Fox's *Book of Martyrs* and a novel of Bandello's, given in Fox. It belonged to the Chamberlain's company, as stated in the entry in the Stationers' books 11th August 1602. It was printed with W. S. on the title-page in 1613. One line is repeated from the *London Prodigal*. This play may be by the same author (T. Lodge?).

Entered 1602, for W. Cotton. Editions: Q. 1, 1602, for W. Jones; Q. 2, 1613, by Thomas Snodham.

A YORKSHIRE TRAGEDY. 1605-8.

This play is in one act, being one portion of *All's One, or Four Plays in One*, played at the Globe.

It is founded on a pamphlet, published in 1605 by V. S[immes], relating a murder, also mentioned in Stow's *Chronicles*, which was committed in that year. In power this is the most remarkable of the doubtful plays. Yet surely Shakespeare could not have written such a production, even for an ephemeral purpose, so late in his career. It has been assigned to Heywood, absurdly; be did not write for the Globe at this time. Tourneur and Jonson did, so did perhaps Beaumont and Fletcher. There is at present no ground for asserting the authorship positively. It was printed with Shakespeare's name in full on the title; but T. Pavier was the printer.

The first scene introduces talk among the servants, 'about my young mistress' who was clearly intended to play a considerable part. She is never heard of afterwards. And no characters in the rest of the play have any names, but these servants have. They pun like Shakespeare. Did he write this first scene and Beaumont the rest of the play? The other instance we have of *Four Plays in One* is by Beaumont and Fletcher—one scene imitates the interference of the servant in *Lear*, III, vii. The two lines,

> ' Divines and dying men may talk of hell,
> But in my heart her several torments dwell,'

occur in the poem at the beginning of Nash's *Piers Penniless*, 1592, and also in the *Insatiate Countess*, by Marston and Barksted, published 1613.

Editions: Q. 1, 1608, R. B[onian], for T. Pavier; Q. 2, 1619, do., do.

THE MERRY DEVIL OF EDMONTON. *Before* 1608.

A Globe play by T. B., as entered by Joseph Hunt and Thomas Archer, 5th April 1608. It was very popular; Jonson calls it the 'dear delight' of the public. H. Moseley entered it as Shakespeare's in 1653.
Editions: Q. 1, 1608, Henry Ballard, for Arthur Johnson; Q. 2, 1612; Q. 3, 1617, G. Eld, for do.; Q. 4, 1626, A. M., for Francis Faulkner; Q. 5, 1631, T. P[avier], for do.; Q. 6, 1655, for William Gilbertson.

THE BIRTH OF MERLIN; OR, THE CHILD HATH FOUND HIS FATHER.

This play was published in 1662, as written by William Shakespeare and William Rowley. It was probably founded on *Uter Pendragon*, a play produced by the Admiral's company 29th April 1597; or on *Valtiger*, also produced by the same company, 4th December 1596. There is not a particle of evidence for attributing this play to Shakespeare. Publishers from 1659 to 1662 put any name upon title-pages that suited their convenience. We do not know the company that owned this production. It was not written by Rowley for the Globe. The only times he was connected with that theatre were in 1607, and in 1623-5; and in 1607, only indirectly through Wilkins, if at all. He may have refashioned it from an old play, for some other company. Three other plays in 1653, and three in 1660, were entered in Shakespeare's name, in the Stationers' books, none of which are extant.
Edition: 1662, Thomas Johnson, for Francis Kirkman and Henry Marsh.

THE FIRST AND SECOND PARTS OF THE TROUBLESOME REIGN OF KING JOHN. *c.* 1591.

This play was acted by the Queen's company. It was probably written by G. Peele, *c.* 1590. The first edition was anonymous. In 1611 'W. Sh.' was put on the title-page to deceive the public, as Shakespeare's play was not then published. Still later, 'W. Shakespeare' was inserted in full. For Shakespeare's use of this play see under *John*.
Editions: Q. 1, 1591, for S. Clarke; Q. 2, 1611, V. S[immes], for J. Helme; Q. 3, by A. Mathews, for T. Dewe, 1622.

FIRST PART OF SIR JOHN OLDCASTLE. 1599.

This play was printed with Shakespeare's name in full on the title-page, for the dishonest bookseller, T. Pavier. It was written for the Admiral's company by Munday, Drayton, Wilson, and Hathaway, in 1599. It was evidently intended to keep in the mind of the public the fact that Shakespeare had represented the Lollard martyr as a coward and jester, in his *Henry IV*.

Editions: Q. 1, 1600, for T. P[avier]; Q. 2, V. [Simmes], for T. Pavier. F. 3, F. 4.

THE PURITAN; OR, THE WIDOW OF WATLING STREET. 1606.

Certainly not Shakespeare's; published with the initials W. S., in 1607. Written for the Children of Paul's, by an Oxford graduate; founded on the *Jests* ascribed to George Peele. Peele (a baker's shovel) is called Pyeboard in this play—one among many proofs of personal allusions hidden under names of characters in these productions. For the date of production, see under *Pericles*, p. 28.

Edition: 1607, by G. Eld. F. 3, F. 4.

THE TRUE TRAGEDY OF RICHARD III. *c.* 1593.

This play is certainly by two hands. The entry of Richmond (sc. xiv) marks the point where the second hand is introduced. It is a poor play. It belonged to the Queen's men, and may have been partly written by Robert Greene.

Edition: Q. 1, by T. Creede.

THE TRUE CHRONICLE HISTORY OF KING LEIR. 1593.

This play was acted by the Queen's and Lord Sussex's men together at the Rose in 1593. It was first printed in 1605, by Simeon Stafford, for John Wright. Its only interest to us is its connection with Shakespeare's play, for which see under *Lear*. Peele was possibly the author of it.

Edition: Q. 1, by S. Stafford, for J. Wright, 1605.

WARNING FOR FAIR WOMEN.

A murder play.
Edition: Q. 1, V. Sims, for W. Aspley, 1599.

'LARUM FOR LONDON; OR, SIEGE OF ANTWERP.

Plot from *The Tragical History of the City of Antwerp*.
Edition: Q. 1, 1602.

CHAPTER V.

HOW SHOULD SHAKESPEARE BE READ?

INDEPENDENTLY of all questions of understanding the text critically and historically, the following points require attention.

I. The pronunciation in Shakespeare's time differed from ours.

- *i* long had two sounds,
  - 1. *i* in t*i*me.
  - *2. *i* in mach*i*ne.
- *e* long had two sounds,
  - *1. *e* in w*e*re.
  - 2. *e* in *e*ve.
- *a* long had three sounds,
  - *1. *a* in f*a*ther.
  - 2. *a* in m*a*re.
  - *3. *a* in *a*ll.
- *o* long had two sounds,
  - 1. *o* in h*o*me.
  - *2. *o* in d*o*.
- *u* long had one sound,
  - 1. *u* in fl*u*te.
- *ai* (*ay*) had two sounds,
  - 1. *ai* in p*ai*l.
  - 2. *ai* in *ai*sle.
- *ei* (*ey*) had two sounds,
  - 1. *ei* in n*ei*gh.
  - *2. *ei* in h*ei*ght.
- *oi* (*oy*) had two sounds,
  - 1. *oi* in *oi*l.
  - *2. *i* in *i*sle.
- *ui* (*uy*) had two sounds,
  - 1. *u* in r*u*le.
  - *2. *i* in *i*sle.
- *ou* (*ow*) had two sounds,
  - 1. *ow* in l*ow*.
  - *2. *ou* in y*ou*.
- *eo* had two sounds,
  - 1. *eo* in p*eo*ple.
  - 2. *eo* in y*eo*man.
- *ea* had three sounds,
  - *1. *ea* in gr*ea*t.
  - 2. *ea* in b*ea*t.
  - 3. *ea* in d*ea*d.

The asterised sounds were much commoner then than now. They require special attention.

- *i* short had one sound,
  - 1. *i* in b*i*ll.
- *e* short had two sounds,
  - 1. *e* in d*e*ll.
  - 2. *i* in b*i*ll.

ă short had two sounds, { 1. *a* in r*a*n.
                           2. *e* in d*e*ll.
ŏ short had two sounds, { 1. *o* in d*o*ll.
                           2. *a* in r*a*n.
ŭ short had one sound,   1. *u* in p*u*ll.
The *u* in b*u*t was not known at that date.

It must specially be noticed that the pronunciation was very unsettled at that time: we find t*a*tter and t*o*tter, b*oi*l and b*i*le, wh*e*ther and wh*i*ther, m*a*n and m*o*n, th*e*n and th*a*n, j*ui*ce and j'ice, n*ow* (like *au*, German) and n*ow* (like n*oo*), indiscriminately used. Thousands of similar instances might be given. Any attempt to fix one pronunciation for every word separately, however elaborate, must necessarily fail.

In consonants the chief points worth noting here are the exceptional pronunciations of *th* sounded as *t* in *moth* (pronounced *mote*), *the* (pronounced *t'*), *those* (pronounced *ta*), *nothing* (pronounced *noting*), and the like; *s* pronounced as *sh*, as *suitor* (pronounced *shooter*); *-tion*, *-sion*, pronounced with a distinct sound of *s*, as *nation*, *patience*, *fusion* (pronounced *na-si-on*, *pa-si-ence*, *fu-si-on*); *ch* pronounced *j*, as *beseech* (pronounced *besiege*); *gh* omitted, and sometimes pronounced *f*, as in *daughter* (which varies between *da'ter*, *dafter*, and *daughiter*, with the guttural sound); *thought* (pronounced *thoft*), etc.

The following general laws may also be laid down:

1. Letters that can be trilled may be made to form a separate syllable; thus, *fire* may be pronounced *fi-er*; *mile*, *mi-el*; *surely*, *su-er-ly*; *haply*, *hap-i-ly*.

Conversely: the flat spirants *th*, *v*, may be omitted altogether in pronunciation; *sevennight* becoming *se'nnight*; *love*, *lo'e*; *give*, *gi'e*; *with*, *wi'*; *whither*, *whi'er*; *corsive*, *corsi'e*, etc. This occasionally happens in other consonants, as *taken*, *ta'en*; notably in *o' th'*, for *on the*; *i' th'*, for *in the*.

2. Any two consecutive consonants may be separated so as to give rise to a new syllable, thus, *heard* may be pronounced *hearŭd*; *grace*, *gĕrace*; *kinsman*, *kinĭsman*. Occasionally this results from the reviving of a vowel that originally existed in the word, as in *Worcĕster*, *commandĕment*, and the like.

Conversely: two syllables ending in the same consonant may be run into one, provided only a short vowel intervenes between the two similar consonants; this is specially noticeable with *t*, *d*, *s*, etc. (dentals): thus, *let it*, may be sounded *let'*; *committed*, *commit'*; *needed*, *need'*; *horses*, *hor se'*; *this is*, *this'*; etc.

3. Any diphthongal sound, or sound involving a consonantal *y* or *w*, may be resolved into two: thus, *swain* may become *soo-ain; twelve, too-elve; joy, jaw-ee; bound, ba-oond*, etc.

Conversely: any two vowel-sounds coming together may be glided into one (not slurred over), by an *appoggiatura*, as in the pronunciation of Italian: thus, *gently͜ away* may be reckoned as three syllables. This is to be specially noticed in contractions (falsely so called), as *I͜ have*, not *I've* (it is always written *I ha'* in the old editions); *he͜ has*, not *he's;* and in the endings in *-ion*, as *dimensi͜ on* (almost *syoon*), not *dimensun* or *dimenshun*.

II. The metre must be attended to; and the following laws noted:

1. In uncorrupted Shakespeare you will find lines of one, two, three, five, and six feet, but never of four feet, unless such lines as can be broken into two of the kinds already mentioned, thus:

4 feet. { A brother's murder (2 feet).
         Pray can I not (2 feet).
4 feet. { But yet they could have wished (3 feet).
         They know not (1 foot).

Nor does he admit lines deficient by an initial syllable, thus, in

'Twelve years since, Miranda, twelve years since,'

the first *twelve* is *too-elve* (not the first *years, yee-ars*, as the editors give it).

2. Wherever a full stop or colon occurs in the middle of a line, Shakespeare treats the line as if composed of two short ones; allows the first part of it to end with an extra syllable (feminine ending), begins the second part with a trochee, and so on, thus:

' To͜ unsta|ble slight|*ness*. || Púrpose | so barred | it fol|*lows*.'

Here we have *to un-* glided into one syllable; *-ness* and *-lows* extra syllables, or feminine endings, as at the end of lines; *purpose* a trochaic foot.

In other matters he follows the usual laws, except that his six-foot lines (Alexandrines) in his later plays often have no cæsura after the third foot.

' A sove|reign chance | so el|||bows him | his own | unkind|ness.'

This statement is denied by the metrists; but it is true.

D

III. Specialities in grammar cannot of course be noticed here; a few general rules may be.

1. When a dissyllabic adjective accented on the last syllable comes before a noun accented on the first, its accent is thrown back, thus: *The man is compléte;* but, *This is a cómplete man.*

2. Adjectives are often used as concrete nouns, thus: *the learned's wing; well, my legitimate; wrinkled old,* etc.

3. Adjectives often take the place of the first part of a compound noun formed from two nouns, thus: *a bloody fire* for 'a blood-fire,' or 'fire in the blood;' *a fruitful prognostication,* for 'a fruit-prognostication,' or 'prophecy of fruitfulness.' Hence the apparent inversion of noun and adjective, as in *living torment,* for 'life-torment,' or 'tormented life;' *murderous shame* for 'murder-shame,' or 'shameful murder.' (*See* 14.)

4. Abbott notices that adjectives are often used for adverbs, but does not notice that conversely adverbs are used for adjectives, thus: *We have safely found our king,* for 'We have found our king safe.' *Lucius' banishment was wrongfully,* for 'wrongful.'

5. The gerund is often used in a passive sense when it occurs not in the predicate but as an attributive, thus: *Women are angels, wooing,* that is, 'in wooing,' 'when wooed;' *By deed-achieving honour newly named,* that is, 'by honour achieved by deeds.'

6. Suffixes and prefixes sometimes apply not only to the word to which they are attached, but also to other words connected by a conjunction, thus: *Sad or merrily*=(sad or merry)-ly=sadly or merrily. *Earth and sea's*=(earth and sea)'s=earth's and sea's. *Revived and breathed*=re(-vived and breathed)=revived and rebreathed. *Fox and lambskins*=(fox and lamb)skins=foxskins and lambskins.

7. Zeugma and syllepsis. Zeugma of the verb: *Or in the ocean drencht or in the fire,* for 'burnt in the fire.' Zeugma of the noun: *A sister I bequeath you, whom no brother did ever love so dearly,* for 'whom I love as never brother loved his.' Syllepsis of the verb auxiliary: *You must be so too if heed me,* for 'if you will heed me.' Inversely: *Many have and others must sit there,* for 'have sat.' Syllepsis of the preposition: *From whence thou mayst come and part,* for 'whither thou mayest come and whence depart.' In all these and similar instances, a word is joined to several others, that naturally refers only to one of them.

8. Prolepsis. *To chase the ignorant fumes that mantle*

their clearer reason, for 'to chase the fumes that mantle their reason, and so make it clearer.' Here an effect is represented in the inserted epithet as already produced, although it has to be produced afterwards.

9. Cumulation. This includes all instances of double negatives, repetitions of inflexions, duplications of expression by an inflexion and a preposition, and the like. Common instances are: 'He did not never do it;' 'the house of Mr Smith's;' 'most highest;' 'from whence;' such names as 'Wans-beck-water,' etc. In Shakespeare the usual form is that of the double negative: *He denied you had in him no right; Let his lack of years be no impediment to let him lack a reverend estimation; You less know how to value her than she to scant her duty.* We should say, 'any right;' 'let him obtain;' 'She is less likely to scant her duty than you to undervalue her.'

10. The use of words in two senses where no pun or comic effect is intended. *Give my love fame faster than time wastes life;* fast=(1) firmly, (2) swiftly. *So sound as hearts that are hollow;* sound=(1) whole, (2) clear-sounding. By a similar reference to preceding words Shakespeare abstracts one part of speech out of another. *They that have power to hurt, and will do none,* that is, 'do no hurt.' *The king loves you; beware you lose it not,* that is, 'lose the love.' *No lesser of her honour confident than I did truly find her,* that is, 'find her honourable.'

11. Use of the abstract for the concrete. *Go, tenderness of years,* that is, 'tender-yeared one.'

12. Concrete for abstract. *He speaks nothing but madman,* that is, 'madness.'

13. The name of a thing for one of its attributes, thus: *His lays were tuned like the lark,* that is, 'like the lark's lays.' *Her dowry shall weigh equal with a queen,* that is, 'with a queen's dowry.'

14. Transposition of words. This is peculiarly Shakespearian, as he uses it to excess:

a. Epithets transposed from subject or predicate to the object, etc., thus: *That pay the willing loan,* that is, 'pay willingly.' *The thrifty hire I saved,* that is, 'I, being thrifty, saved.' *Course of direct session,* that is, 'direct course of session.'

b. Interchange of adjectival and substantival words. *Nature's truth*=true nature. *Habit's devil*=devilish habit. Inversely: *Your word's deceit* = your deceitful words. *Heart-wisht luxury*=luxurious desire.

c. Inversion of the whole idea. *Hell of time* = time of hell. *Put fear to valour* = put valour to fear. *More to know did never meddle with my thoughts* = my thoughts did never meddle with knowing more.

All these grammatical remarks are taken (with a few alterations) from Schmidt's excellent *Shakespeare Lexicon.* For special details see Abbott's *Shakespearian Grammar.* These two books are worth all the commentaries on Shakespearian language put together.

CHAPTER VI.

WHO ACTED PLAYS IN SHAKESPEARE'S TIME?

The principal companies of actors in Shakespeare's time may be conveniently treated of in groups.

1. The Children of Paul's, who acted in their own Convocation Room from 1563 to 1589, when they were suspended, and from 1601 to c. 1606.

2. The Children of Westminster acted 1567-75; the Children of Windsor, 1571-7. The Children of the Chapel outlasted both these companies, acting 1565-1603. During the latter part of this time, 1596-1603, they occupied the Blackfriars Theatre, which was let out by Burbadge to one Evans. In 1603-4 they became the Children of the Revels; c. 1610 they left Blackfriars, which was then appropriated by the King's company, and went to Whitefriars, where they stayed till 1613. Whether they were afterwards formed into the Duke of York's (Prince Charles's) company is doubtful. But that company is first heard of when these children leave Blackfriars. The Lady Elizabeth's company (1613-22) were also closely connected with Prince Charles (the first's) company.

3. Philip Howard, Earl of Arundel, had a company which played from 1574 to 1584. Lord Charles Howard, Lord Admiral and Earl of Nottingham, had a company, probably the same, which played from 1585 to 1589, when it was suspended; it recommenced in 1593. In 1603 its title was changed to that of the servants of Prince Henry; on his death in 1612, they became the Palsgrave's men.

4. Lord Darby (Stanley) had a company from 1582 to 1584. Ferdinand Stanley, Lord Strange, had a company, probably the same, from 1589 to 1594; they then became the Lord Chamberlain's. They were after 1603 called the King's servants. During the short time that William Brooke, Lord Cobham, was chamberlain (August 1596 to April 1597) they were called Lord Hunsdon's servants.

5. From 1562 to 1582 Lord Robert Dudley had a company; after his accession to the title of Earl of Leicester, they were generally called the Earl of Leicester's men. Sir Robert

Lane had a company from 1571 to 1573. The Earl of Warwick (J. Dudley) had also a company in 1564. These two last-named united in 1574, and were called the Earl of Warwick's men till 1582. In 1583 the Earl of Warwick's and the Earl of Leicester's companies were dissolved, and Queen Elizabeth's men were formed out of them. There was only one Queen's company in Elizabeth's time, not two as usually stated. They broke up in 1593. The Earl of Worcester's company were formed *c.* 1601, certainly were playing in 1602. In 1603 they took the name of Queen Anne's men, and retained it till her death in 1619.

6. Henry Cary, Lord Hunsdon, had a company from 1582 to 1586. They were probably the same as the subsequent company of Lord Strange.

The Earl of Sussex (J. Ratcliff) had a company which played from 1576 to 1583, and from 1591 to 1594.

William Herbert, Earl of Pembroke, had a company from 1592 to 1600.

William Stanley, Lord Darby, had a company from 1599 to 1600.

These three last-named companies were closely connected, and were all probably united with or absorbed in the Chamberlain's or other companies.

CHAPTER VII.

WHERE WERE PLAYS ACTED IN SHAKESPEARE'S TIME?

1. THE Children of Paul's had a private room of their own in their Convocation house; certainly used for this purpose, from 1575 onwards.

2. The earliest theatre proper was the Theater in Shoreditch, which was built by James Burbadge in 1576. The Queen's company probably acted in it to 1593; Sussex's and Pembroke's till 1597. It was closed in 1598; pulled down by the younger Burbadges, and the materials used in building the Globe in 1599.

3. The Globe on Bankside was built in 1599. The Chamberlain's company (afterwards the King's) acted here always. It was burnt in 1613, but rebuilt the same year.

4. The Crosskeys tavern in Grace Church Street (Gracious Street), was used as a winter house by the company of Lord Strange, from 1589 to 1594.

5. Blackfriars Theatre was built, or rather rebuilt, by the Burbadges in 1596. They let it out to one Evans, who placed the Chapel Children in it from 1596 to 1603. In 1603-4 this company took the name of the Children of the Revels, and remained there till *c*. 1610. These children having grown up to be men, the Burbadges bought the remainder of the lease, and set up in it 'Shakespeare, Heminge, Condell, and other deserving men:' it was used as well as the Globe by the King's company from that time onwards.

6. Whitefriars Theatre was occupied by the Children of the Revels from the time of their leaving Blackfriars to 1613: after that date we hear nothing of it.

7. The Cockpit, Phœnix, or private house in Drury Lane, was built *c*. 1616, and occupied by Queen Anne's company till 1619; then by the Lady Elizabeth's company. There was also a Cockpit at court (Whitehall); these must be carefully distinguished.

8. The Hope on Bankside had been previously occupied by the Lady Elizabeth's men in 1614.

9. The Curtain, in Shoreditch, was built immediately after the Theater in 1576. It was probably occupied by the Admiral's men 1583-9; by Pembroke's 1589-92; by Lord Strange's in 1593; and by the Lord Chamberlain's 1594-9. It was then, perhaps, taken by Lord Darby's men. In 1603 Queen Anne's company played there, and remained there till 1616.

10. The Red Bull tavern in St John's Street, was generally used by the same company as the Curtain. Queen Elizabeth's company played there, also Queen Anne's.

11. The Rose Theatre on Bankside was opened by Henslow 1592. We can give the exact dates for the companies that acted here from his *Diary:*

Lord Strange's,	. .	19th Feb. 1592 to 1st Feb. 1593.
Earl of Sussex's,	. .	27th Dec. 1593 to 6th Feb. 1594.
Sussex's and Queen's,	.	1st April 1594 to 8th April 1594.
Admiral's,	. . .	14th May 1594 to 28th July 1597.
Admiral's and Pembroke's,		11th Oct. 1597 to 5th Nov. 1597.
Admiral's,	. . .	5th Nov. 1597 to 20th June 1600.
Worcester's,	. . .	17th Aug. 1602 to 16th March 1603.

The Chamberlain's *may* have acted here a few days in June 1594.

12. There was a building at Newington Butts, at which the Chamberlain's men (possibly the Admiral's), acted from 3d June 1594, for a few days.

13. The Fortune Theatre, Golden Lane, Whitecross Street, was built by Ned Alleyn in 1600. The Admiral's company went there in September of that year from the Rose. After the death of Prince Henry, this company, then called by his name, became the Palsgrave's. They still remained here. This theatre was square; when rebuilt after its burning in 1621, it was made round. The Globe also was round.

The Swan on Bankside; Paris Garden; Belle Savage, Ludgate Hill; and Boar's Head, were occupied sometimes for dramatic performances. No theatre of note was built after Shakespeare's death before the closing of all of them in 1642, except Salisbury Court in Whitefriars.

There were also frequently performances at court.

CHAPTER VIII.

WHO WERE SHAKESPEARE'S CONTEMPORARIES?

IN order to understand Shakespeare's position as a dramatist it is necessary to know who besides him were writing for the stage; and if any further study of the drama of his time be intended by the reader, it will be necessary for him frequently to refer to the lives of these writers. I have, therefore, endeavoured to extract the facts known about the chief of these dramatists from the lengthy criticisms in which they are in almost all cases embedded, and to give them here apart from lists of their works, which are better for our purpose treated separately. Those not mentioned here, such as Kyd, Haughton, Porter, and the like, we know absolutely nothing of apart from their works. Indeed, with the exception of Jonson, hardly any dramatist of that time has what is worthy to be called a biography.

Perhaps the following scheme may serve as an approximate classification for the period before Shakespeare's death:

Lyly,
Greene, } Pamphleteering group.
Nash,

Marlow,
Peele, } Shakespearian group.
Lodge,

Marston,
Chapman, } Writers for children's companies (mostly).
Middleton,

Heywood,
Webster, } Writers for men's companies (mostly).
Dekker,

Jonson,
Tourneur,
Beaumont, } Globe group.
Fletcher,

Field,
Rowley, } Actor-writers.

Chettle, . . ⎫
Haughton, . . ⎬ Rose group.
Munday, . . ⎪
Porter, . . ⎭

LYLY.

John Lyly was born in Kent in 1553-4. He matriculated in Magdalen College, Oxford, as *plebeii filius* in 1571; was, for his satire, rusticated, but made B.A. 27th April 1573; M.A. 1st June 1575. On 16th May 1574, he wrote to Lord Burghley for help and patronage at Oxford. In March 1577, Benger, the Master of the Revels, died, and Lyly wrote to the queen to remind her of her promise made ten years since (in 1567), to give him the reversion. In July 1579 E. Tylney was appointed. Lyly then wrote again saying he had been thirteen years at court and got nothing (was this *plebeii filius* at court at twelve years old before going to Oxford? These dates are a puzzle). It appears from his first letter that he had written plays before 1576. If so, he must have produced his *Woman in the Moon*, his first play, before that date. This satire on the queen would quite account for his disgrace. He writes again to Burghley in July 1582 to excuse himself from dishonesty and irreverence towards her. It was not published till 1597. In 1589 he published his *Pap with a Hatchet* in the Mar-prelate controversy. He was replied to by Gabriel Harvey, who was in turn answered by T. Nash. He died after 1597. He was short, and a great smoker. All his plays must have been produced before 1589, as the Children of Paul's, who acted them, were suspended from that year till 1601. He was praised by W. Webbe (*Discourse of English Poetry*), 1586; by Henry Upchear (*Menaphon*), 1589; I. Elliott (*Perimedes*), 1588; Lodge (*Wit's Misery*), 1596; Meres (*Palladis Tamia*), 1598; in *Alisda*, 1616; and Jonson's memorial verses to Shakespeare, 1623. Harvey was obliged to admit his public reputation (*Pierce's Supererogation*), 1593; on the other hand the style of his *Euphues*, 1580-1, was ridiculed by Drayton, Marston (*What You Will*), 1607, and Jonson (*Cynthia's Revels*), 1600; if not by Shakespeare in his *Love's Labour's Lost*. Spenser's allusion to our 'pleasant Willy dead of late,' probably refers to Lyly. He was satirised in various plays from 1591 to 1601. Shakespeare imitated many passages from him, and adopted his manner of punning in and out of season.

ROBERT GREENE.

Greene was born at Norwich c. 1550; became B.A. of St John's College, Cambridge, 1578; M.A. of Clare Hall 1583; incorporated at Oxford 1583. He then went to Spain, Italy, Germany, Poland, Denmark. He may have been the Robert Greene who was queen's chaplain, and presented by her to the rectory of Walkington, in York diocese, on 1st August 1576. He was still more likely presented to the vicarage of Tollesbury, in Essex, 19th June, which he resigned the next year to come to London as a playwright and penner of love pamphlets. He married an amiable woman who bore him a child. He then abandoned her. There was a Greene, *alias* Wilde, who married one Elizabeth Taylor, 16th February 1586; was this our Greene? His associates at this time were Marlow, Peele, and Lodge. He quarrelled with them before 1589, and became the companion and fellow-in-arms of T. Nash in the pamphlet war then going on. At the same time he gave up play-writing. He had also been an actor. In August 1592, he at an entertainment with Nash ate too much pickled herring, and drank too much Rhenish wine. This produced an illness which killed him. A shoemaker near Dowgate, desperately poor, had taken him in, and he and his wife nursed him. Not one of his friends came near him. Two women did. One, not the forsaken wife, but the sister of Cutting Ball, the mother of his illegitimate son, Fortunatus Greene : the other a Mistress Appleby. He died 3d September 1592, desiring that his hostess would crown his corpse with a garland of bays, and was buried at the New Churchyard near Bedlam, on 4th September 1592. His last letter was to his wife, after six years' desertion: 'Doll, I charge thee by the love of our youth and my soul's rest, that thou wilt see this man paid; for if he and his wife had not succoured me, I had died in the streets.—Robert Greene.' He had long red hair, and was of scholarly and amiable appearance. He wrote for the Queen's players. Much autobiography is contained in his prose works, especially in *Never too late to Mend*, 1590, the *Groatsworth of Wit*, 1592, the *Repentance of Robert Greene*, 1592. His *Dorastus and Fawnia* is the groundwork of Shakespeare's *Winter's Tale*. His enmity to Shakespeare has been noticed already.

THOMAS NASH.

Thomas Nash, son of William Nash, minister, and Margaret his wife, was baptized at Lowestoft, in Suffolk, November 1567. He was admitted a scholar of St John's, Cambridge, on Lady Margaret's foundation, in 1584, proceeded B.A. 1585, was probably expelled, travelled in Italy, and came to London in 1589. He at once rushed into the Marprelate controversy, joined Greene in his literary squabbles, wrote tracts against Gabriel Harvey, and a comedy for the Chapel Children, 1592; got imprisoned for his *Isle of Dogs*, written for the Admiral's company, 1597; and died before 1601. He was the greatest master of satirical abuse that then existed. He was also employed to finish a tragedy of Marlow's in 1594, for the Chapel Children.

CHRISTOPHER MARLOW.

On 26th February 1564, Christopher, son of John Marlow, was christened in the church of St George the Martyr, Canterbury. John was probably a shoemaker, and at his death, in 1605, was clerk of St Mary's. Christopher was at King's School from Michaelmas 1578 to Michaelmas 1579. In 1580 he was entered (as Marlin) at Benet (Corpus Christi), Cambridge. On 17th March 1581 he matriculated as pensioner, proceeded B.A. 1583, commenced M.A. 1587. He probably came to London in 1584. In May 1593 he was killed in a tavern brawl at Deptford, by Francis Archer, and buried in St Nicholas' Church, on 1st June. He was accused of atheism by his contemporaries, but this was a wide term in those days. He wrote for the Admiral's company till 1589; after that date for Pembroke's and Lord Strange's. He was the founder of our dramatic blank verse system, and the greatest master of tragedy of his time.

GEORGE PEELE.

Peele was a gentleman by birth, a native of Devonshire, born 1558. Student of Christ Church, Oxford, *c.* 1573; B.A. 12th June 1577; M.A. 6th July 1579. He went to London in 1581. He had some land in right of his wife. He was actor, poet, and playwright. When Albertus Alasco, Polish Prince Palatine, visited Oxford in June 1583, Peele was concerned in providing a comedy and a tragedy for the occasion. They were written by Dr Gager. Besides plays Peele wrote some verses for pageants, etc., of small interest. He first wrote for the Chapel Children, 1584, then for other companies till 1589, when he joined the Queen's company. In

INTRODUCTION TO SHAKESPEARIAN STUDY. 61

1591 he wrote for Pembroke's; from 1592 onwards for Lord Strange's, afterwards the Chamberlain's. On 17th January 1595-6 he wrote to Lord Burleigh *Parens Patriæ;* sent him his *Tale of Troy* 'by his eldest daughter, Necessity's servant,' and represented his sickness and poverty. This was doubtless his last illness. He was dead before 1598.

THOMAS LODGE.

Thomas Lodge was the second son of Sir Thomas Lodge, Lord Mayor of London, whose wife was Anne, the daughter of Sir William Laxton. He was born *c.* 1556; was a servitor of Trinity College, Oxford, in 1573, and educated under Sir Edward Hoby. Stephen Gosson, *c.* 1582, calls him a 'vagrant person,' but he was certainly not an actor. In 1584 he was a student of Lincoln's Inn. He became a soldier before 1590, and had sailed with Captain Clarke to the Canaries and Terceras. He also was sailing with Cavendish to the Straits of Magellan from 26th August 1591 to 11th June 1593. He had a house at Low Layton, 5th November 1596. He then studied medicine at Avignon; and became a doctor; and died of the plague in 1625. Before 1589 he had written a play for the Admiral's company, and joined Greene in another for the Queen's. He then ostensibly retired from the stage, but, in my opinion, continued to write anonymously for it till at least 1610. He wrote medical works, a satire, translations, etc., besides *Rosalynd,* noticed under Shakespeare's *As You Like It.*

JOHN MARSTON.

John Marston was born *c.* 1575, probably in Coventry. He became a commoner or gentleman-commoner of Brasenose College, Oxford, in 1591; was admitted B.A. February 1593, as the eldest son of an esquire, and soon after 'went his way.' His father was probably John Marston, a counsellor, who was appointed lecturer of the Middle Temple in 1592. Marston, the dramatist, married Mary, daughter of the Rev. William Wilkes, chaplain to James I, and rector of Barford St Martin, Wiltshire. He died 25th June 1634, and was buried in the Temple Church near his father. Jonson says, in his conversations with Drummond, that Marston wrote his father-in-law's preachings, and his father-in-law his comedies; also, that 'he had many quarrels with Marston, beat him, and took his pistol from him; wrote his

Poetaster on him; the beginning of them were, that Marston represented him in the stage, in his youth given to venerie.' His connection with *Eastward Ho!* will be noticed under Jonson. He wrote one play for the Admiral's at the Rose in 1599, one for the Paul's Children in 1601-2, after this six plays, all for the Revels Children, 1602-7.

GEORGE CHAPMAN.

This poet was born in 1559, as we learn from the portrait prefixed to his *Homer*, at or near Hitchin Hill, in Hertfordshire. See his *Euthymiæ Raptus*, 1609: 'In thy native air, and on the hill next Hitchin's left hand.' He studied for a while at Oxford, but took no degree. He was patronised by Sir Thomas Walsingham and his son, by Henry, Prince of Wales, and by the favourite Somerset. Jonson 'loved him.' Antony Ward calls him 'a person of most reverend aspect, religious and temperate, qualities rarely meeting in a poet.' He died in London, 12th May 1634, and was buried at St Giles in the Fields. As a dramatist, he wrote first for the Admiral's company at the Rose, 1598-9; then for the Children of Paul's, 1601-2; then for the Children of the Revels, 1603-13. The plays, in which Shirley is supposed to have written with him, were more likely altered by the younger dramatist at their revival. *Alphonsus of Germany* is not by him.

In 1605 he was in great distresses:

1. He was or had been imprisoned, with Jonson and Marston, for his share in writing *Eastward Ho!* produced 1603-4.

2. He was in prison with Jonson about a play (name unknown), writing as to which Jonson mentions 'my former error!'

3. He was impeached by the French ambassador as to his *Byron's Conspiracy*, in which he had introduced the French queen as giving Mademoiselle de Verneuil a box on the ear. Three actors were arrested for this play, but the author escaped. So writes the French ambassador, 5th April 1605. It is difficult to believe that Chapman should have been in difficulty for three plays in one year. I would therefore identify the first and second of these troubles, and refer Jonson's 'former error' to his having written part of *Byron's Conspiracy*. There were certainly two hands in this play; part of the last act cannot be by Chapman. In this case we should have only one imprisonment, and a reason for Jonson's

INTRODUCTION TO SHAKESPEARIAN STUDY. 63

not mentioning the second pen in *Sejanus*, which he published this same year, if that second pen was Chapman, as I believe. As the year began 25th March, surely this matter of the *Byron* play must have been the earliest of these troubles in or before 1605, and Gifford says Jonson and Chapman were released from prison in the *Eastward Ho!* matter, early in that year.

THOMAS MIDDLETON.

Born *c.* 1574, in South London; was educated as a gentleman; served a short time in the wars in France or the Netherlands. Probably belonged to Cambridge University, and became a member of Gray's Inn in 1593; appointed chronologer to the city of London 1620; died 1627. He wrote for the Admiral's company in 1602; for the Paul's Children, 1602-4; for Prince Henry's, *c.* 1604-7; for the Revels Children, *c.* 1607-8; then for Lady Elizabeth's; then for Prince Charles's, *c.* 1611-15; finally for the King's, 1616-26. In 1624 he represented on the stage in his *Game at Chess*, James I, the King of Spain, Gondomar, the Bishop of Spalato, and others. For this the play was prohibited, and the players bound over in £300, but no punishment was inflicted on them, or on the poet.

THOMAS HEYWOOD.

Thomas Heywood was a native of Lincolnshire, and a fellow of Peterhouse, Cambridge. On 14th October 1596, he was writing for the Admiral's company. On 25th March 1598, he was regularly engaged by Henslow as a player and sharer in that house. In 1599 he belonged to Lord Darby's men. He joined the Earl of Worcester's company in 1602, which afterwards became Queen Anne's. From 1626 to 1628 he appears to have been a member of Queen Henrietta's players, and from 1629 to 1633 of the King's. He says he wrote all or great part of two hundred and twenty plays. He could hardly have been born much later than 1570, if, as I believe, he began to write 1594. He died about 1640.

JOHN WEBSTER.

If our John Webster, who was born free of the Merchant Tailors' Company, was son of John Webster, merchant tailor (as is most likely), we may also infer that he lived in Holywell Street among the actors. Also, if he married Isabel Sutton on 25th July 1590, and Alice Webster, his daughter, was baptized at St Leonard's Church, 9th May 1606, then he could not well have been born later than 1574. He died *c.* 1652. In 1601 he was writing or altering a play for the Admiral's company; in 1602 writing for Worcester's; in 1603 for the Paul's Children; *c.* 1603-11 for Queen Anne's; and in 1616 for the King's company. He is the greatest master of the horrible of all the dramatists.

THOMAS DEKKER.

That this poet was born and brought up in London, is known from his prose tract, *The Seven Deadly Sins of London*, 1606, wherein he thus addresses the metropolis : 'From thy womb received I my being, from thy breasts my nourishment.' In his *English Villanies Seven Several Times Prest to Death*, February 1637, he speaks of 'my threescore years.' He was therefore not born later than 1577. If he speaks in round numbers, his birth may be as early as 1572. The last notice of him is 1638. He died probably *c.* 1641. He seems to have been very poor. He wrote for the Admiral's company, 1595-1600; for the Children of Paul's, *c.* 1603; for Queen Anne's company, 1603-4; for Prince Henry's, 1604-8; for the Revels company about 1620; for Prince Charles's about 1623.

BEN JONSON.

Benjamin Jonson was born in 1573, a posthumous child. His father was a minister of the Gospel. His mother married again *c.* 1575. His stepfather was a bricklayer in Hartshorn Lane, near Charing Cross. Ben was sent to a private school in the church of St Martin in the Fields ; afterwards to Westminster, where he was in the class of Camden, then second master. He thence went to St John's, Cambridge, with an exhibition, *c.* 1589. Unable to subsist on it, he came home, and worked at bricklaying for about a year. He then went to Flanders as a volunteer in the army, *c.* 1592 ; and in his one campaign there, had, in the face of both the camps, killed an enemy and taken his *spolia opima* from him. Early in 1593 he most likely married. A Maria Jonson, probably the Mary, the 'daughter of her parents' youth,' of the *Epitaph* written by him, died of the plague and was buried at St Martin's in the Fields, 17th November 1593. He had also a son born in 1596 (see *Epigram* 45), and other sons : Joseph, buried 9th December 1599, at St Giles, Cripplegate ; Benjamin, an infant, buried 1st October 1600, at St Botolph,

Bishopsgate; Benjamin, baptized 20th February 1608, at St Anne's, Blackfriars, buried 18th November 1611; Benjamin, baptized 6th April 1610, at St Martin's in the Fields, died 1635. (Is there not some error as to these Benjamins?)

In 1597 there is a notice of him in Henslow's *Diary;* but in 1598 we find him writing for the Chamberlain's company. In that year he killed Gabriel Spenser, an actor in the Admiral's company, in a duel. In a letter of Henslow's we read: 'Since you were with me I have lost one of my company, which hurteth me greatly, that is Gabriel, for he is slain in Hogesden Fields by the hands of bergemen [Benjamin] Jonson, bricklayer.' Jonson's own account is: 'Since his coming to England being appealed to the Fields, he had killed his adversary, which had hurt him in the arm, and whose sword was 10 inches longer than his; to the which he was imprisoned and almost at the gallows.' Drummond adds: 'Then took he his religion [Roman Catholicism] by trust of a priest who visited him in prison.' Jonson says that spies were set to catch him there, but he was warned by the gaoler. In 1599 he did not return to the Chamberlain's company on his release from prison; but joined the Chapel Children. Until 1602 he was, besides writing for the Admiral's men, engaged in his famous stage-quarrel with Dekker, Marston, and others. In 1603 he returned to the King's company, formerly the Chamberlain's, and wrote his *Sejanus* for it, in company with another hand (? Chapman); he afterwards revised it, entirely omitting his coadjutor's work. Soon after, at latest in 1605, his friends Marston and Chapman were imprisoned for reflections on the Scots, contained in *Eastward Ho!* Jonson, who had written part of the play but not the offensive part, voluntarily joined them. They were released, not without much interest. In 1605 we have a second notice of his being imprisoned with Chapman about a play. Jonson writes to the Earl of Salisbury that: 'Since my first error I have so attempered my style, that I have given no cause to any good man of grief.'

In 1605* Jonson recanted, and returned to the English Church. Henceforth all his plays, with the exception of *Bartholomew Fair*, 1614, seem to have been written for the King's players. Between 1603 and 1605, he had already written some entertainments; but in 1605 he began the series of masques (in which kind he is *facile princeps*) that lasted till 1634. In 1611 he arranged the 'testimonies to the

---

* So Gifford, but query in 1610? He was a papist twelve years.

author's merit,' which were prefixed to *Conyat's Crudities*. In 1615 he finally left his shrewish wife, and went with Sir W. Raleigh's son to the Continent. He afterwards remained with Lord Aubigny. In 1616 he published the first volume of the folio edition of his works. The second folio volume was in no way prepared by him. James I, too, in 1616 gave him 100 marks (£66, 13s. 4d.) pension for life by letters-patent. Daniel, hitherto the court poet, then withdrew from court altogether. In 1618 Jonson went to Scotland on foot, and spent several months about Edinburgh in the houses of the gentry. He gave Taylor, the water poet, a 22s. piece in gold about 20th September. Before 17th January 1619, he visited William Drummond the poet, at Hawthornden. He was back in London on 10th May 1619. He next visited Dr Corbet at Christ Church, Oxford, and was created M.A. 19th July 1619. Cambridge had previously paid him a like honour. He frequently made such visits, and also attended the court in some of their progresses when his masques were performed. On 5th October 1621, the king gave him the reversion of the Mastership of the Revels, and offered him knighthood, which he refused. In 1625 he was attacked by palsy. On 19th January 1630, his *New Inn* was hissed off the stage; soon after Charles I gave him £100. Jonson then sent him a rhymed petition to change his 100 marks pension into 100 pounds. Charles did so, and added a tierce of canary wine. At Christmas 1631-2, Aurelius Townshend was appointed to invent a masque in Jonson's place. This was in consequence of his quarrelling with Inigo Jones. He took his revenge on him in his *Tale of a Tub*, 1633. In September 1628 he had been appointed City Chronologer, in place of Middleton, who died in 1624. In November 1631, the Court of Aldermen withdrew their salary of 100 nobles (£33, 6s. 8d.) till he showed some work done for it. In sickness and want he applied to Lord Treasurer Weston for aid. He received in consequence much help in coin, and many praises in verse. The Earl of Newcastle asked for copies of the latter in February 1632. The part of the *Tale of a Tub* in which he satirised Inigo Jones, was suppressed in 1633. He worked on to the last, and died on 6th August 1637, and was buried on 9th August in Westminster Abbey. He left no wife, no children. He was large-headed, but short of stature, corpulent, and scorbutic. This account of him omits many characteristic particulars for want of space. I ought to add, though, that his house, containing many of his valuable writings in MS., was burnt between 1621 and 1629; and that the Earl of

Pembroke sent him £20 a year for many years to buy books. He was the most solid and learned of all the play-writers.

CYRIL TOURNEUR.

Of this writer nothing is known, but that he wrote for the King's company *c.* 1607-11.

FRANCIS BEAUMONT.

Francis Beaumont, third son of Judge Beaumont, was born at Grace Dieu early in 1586. On 4th February 1597, he was admitted with his two brothers as a gentleman-commoner of Broadgates Hall, Oxford. He entered as a member of the Inner Temple, 3d November 1600; published his *Salmacis and Hermaphroditus* in 1602; wrote some plays by himself, and then joined Fletcher, *c.* 1607. He was a friend of Jonson's at that date. On the death of his brother Henry, in February 1608, he inherited a considerable sum. He was one of the principal wits who met with Jonson and others at the Mermaid, in the club established by Sir W. Raleigh before the end of Elizabeth's reign. He married, *c.* 1613, Ursula, daughter of Henry Islay of Sundridge, in Kent; and died on 6th March 1616. He was buried in Westminster Abbey. After his marriage he appears to have given up play-writing. He left two daughters. The loss to literature by his early death has been compared to that caused by Marlow's, but Beaumont had probably given up writing some years before he died.

JOHN FLETCHER.

John Fletcher was one of the many children of Richard Fletcher, Bishop of London. He was born at Rye, in Sussex, while his father was minister there in December 1579, and was baptized on the 20th of that month. He was admitted pensioner of Bene't College, Cambridge, on 15th October 1591, and Bible clerk in 1593. His father, who died 15th June 1596, left him half his library: *c.* 1607 he joined Beaumont in writing for the King's company. They wrote for the Revels Children from 1611 to 1613. Fetcher after this wrote for the King's company from 1614 till his death in 1625, mostly alone, but, besides altering Shakespeare after 1613, he wrote with Field, Daborne, and Massinger about 1615; with Middleton *c.* 1616-9; with Massinger 1620-2; and Rowley 1623. While working with Beaumont they lived together on the Bankside, and had clothes, etc., in common. He died, August 1625, of the plague, and was buried on the 29th of that month at St Saviour's, Southwark.

NATHANIEL FIELD.

Nathaniel Field was one of the children of the Queen's Chapel, 1600-1; of the Revels Children in 1609-12; of the Prince Henry and Lady Elizabeth companies, united, in 1613; of the King's company, 1618-20. His plays were written 1610-1. His letter, written in the name of Massinger, Daborne, and himself, to Henslow for assistance, was probably written in 1613.

WILLIAM ROWLEY.

William Rowley, like Field, was a player and a playwright. He wrote for the Queen's company at the Curtain in 1607; for the Revels Children before 1613; for Prince Charles's company (of which he was manager, 1613-6) between 1613 and 1623; for the King's company, 1623-6. He also wrote for Lady Elizabeth's and Queen Henrietta's companies, probably c. 1612-3.

HENRY CHETTLE.

Was probably a printer in partnership with J. Danter and William Hoskins. He wrote plays for the Admiral's company between 1598 and 1603.

ANTONY MUNDAY.

Antony Munday was born in 1553. He was a citizen and a draper; in 1589 he lived in Cripplegate. He carried on his business to 1613 at least. He was employed as city poet to write pageants many times between 1599 and 1616. In 1582 he was instrumental in detecting the Popish conspiracy. The Jesuits attacked him as being first a stage-player, then an apprentice, then hissed from the stage, and going to Rome, and then coming back to his original occupation. He admitted having been the Pope's scholar in the Seminary at Rome, but denied having been a Catholic. He began to write in 1579. His plays were written for the Admiral's company between 1597 and 1602. He died 10th August 1633. Most of the poets for the Admiral's company were from the city of London, not from the universities.

CHAPTER IX.

AUTOBIOGRAPHY OF A STAGE PLAY.

I AM an unfortunate tragedy. I was stolen from my true progenitor by a penny poet, who gained his wretched subsistence by cobbling or translating other men's productions. He so mangled my originally fair proportions by patching on excrescences and defacing my natural beauties, that I could scarcely have been recognised by any one but my own parent. From his hands I passed into those of the Master of the Revels, who was chiefly anxious to purge me of all profanity, and utterly careless whether my language were that of a muse, a thinker, or a stealer of scraps of languages. He sent me back to the players, who cut down my proportions to their own uses, so that whereas I had formerly marched on chopines, I now halted in socks. They also taught me many slight asseverations in the place of the mouth-filling oaths that the Revels Master had so vehemently eschewed, and showed me how to tax individuals under pretext of satirising the times. My identity was already sufficiently doubtful, but under the management of a brachygraphist employed by a piratical bookseller, I was so mangled through his slowness of hand, imperfection of hearing, and general dulness of understanding, that on my presentation to the public in my new guise, my reputed father indignantly disowned me, and deprived me of almost the only thing I still retained of my original property, my name. He even at the suggestion of a stage manager, began to dress up a younger son of his to resemble me as far as his art could accomplish it, with the name, guise, and general appearance that I had at first. As, however, he died just at this time, I myself was tricked out by my stepfather some short time after in my younger brother's vestments, with additions to no small extent, from my stepfather's own wardrobe. I now passed for myself, and was supposed to be the same person as at first, restored to my pristine youth and beauty. In this state I expect to die and be embalmed, and in this state to remain until some critic of distant centuries shall dig me up, unswathe my mummy, and carefully assign on undoubted evidence every rag of my surroundings to its original owner, whether it be to my father, to the Master of the Revels, to some of the dozen players or their manager, to my stepfather, or who else. This may, no doubt, with sufficient care, be performed by a critic who has the requisite subtilty, historical knowledge, and acquaintance with the properties of mummy-swathings, chemical, manufactural, or textural, and the results may be tabulated by him with great satisfaction—to himself. Meanwhile, until then, I hope to rest in peace.

The above is intended to aid the memory as to the following facts:

1. Plots of plays were often appropriated. See Kemp's *Nine Days' Wonder*, and compare Shakespeare's *John* and *Lear* with the older plays on which they are founded.

2. The Master of the Revels often cut out objectionable expressions or scenes. Examples: Jonson's *Tale of the Tub;* Davenant's *Wits* (corrected by King Charles I). Compare the quarto and folio editions of 2 *Henry IV* as to the use of oaths, either inserted by players in the quarto, or cut out by the Revels' master in the folio.

3. Editions were often made up by dishonest booksellers, who obtained their versions by short-hand notes made during representation, by employing some penny poet to fill up the gaps. Examples: 2 and 3 *Henry VI*, *Hamlet*, Q. 1, etc. The dramatists often complain of this practice.

4. Actors, especially the clowns, often inserted extempore speeches. This is sometimes indicated by an '&c.' in the printed copies. Example: Marlow's *Tamburlaine;* see *Hamlet*, III, ii, 42.

5. Dramatists often revised and greatly altered (for revivals) their own productions. Examples: *Merry Wives of Windsor;* Jonson's *Every Man in his Humour*.

6. Dramatists often re-wrote the productions of others after the original author's death; sometimes putting their own name to the altered play, sometimes the original writer's, sometimes both. Examples: Marlow's *Faustus*, altered by Rowley and Bird; Fletcher's *Night Walker*, altered by Shirley. This is important, as bearing on the question whether *Macbeth* has been altered.

7. The names of plays were often changed. Examples: Fletcher's *Night Walker;* Massinger's *Tyrant;* Shakespeare's *Love's Labour's Won*.

8. Plays were often greatly condensed for stage purposes. Examples: Fletcher's *Chances;* Marlow's *Massacre of Paris.* Compare *The Tempest, Julius Cæsar,* etc., with other plays, as to length and construction.

9. Authors sometimes re-wrote plays, in which a second hand had originally aided, so as to exclude all work but their own in the revised edition. Example: Jonson's *Sejanus;* compare the two versions of *Romeo and Juliet.*

General conclusion.—As every one of these various alterations have been *demonstrated* in instances where the printers have not noticed them in their editions, we are thrown entirely on *internal* evidence for a basis of judgment as to whether they have been made in other instances, always excepting the cases in which the author superintended the printing of his own work, such as Jonson's first folio, or the Shakespeare quartos before 1600.

CHAPTER X.

HOW WERE SHAKESPEARE'S PLAYS REPRESENTED?

LET us in imagination attend the representation of a play (say of Fletcher's *Bonduca*) at the Blackfriars Theatre, near the end of Shakespeare's career, about 1613. While passing through the streets of wooden houses, half Italian, half Gothic, with overhanging upper stories and projecting oriels, we may note the costumes of the populace. Brown-cassocked soldiers, blue-coated servitors, flat-capped prentices, broken soldiers in rags, sergeants in buff, elbow us on all sides. Sometimes a round-headed black clothed puritan featherdealer of the Blackfriars eyes us with distrust; sometimes a haunter of St Paul's addresses us in the hope of meeting with a gull; sometimes a gallant, who has just paid his spurmoney for entering the cathedral, brushes roughly against us; tailors and laundresses from the Exchange, roaring-boys and cheaters, are abundant in the streets and alleys that we pass through. At last we arrive at our little theatre, snugly roofed in from the weather. How unlike the old Globe, six-sided, brick-coloured, conical, that we used to go to when the Children had the private house! In those days when the red flag was displayed on the pole at its summit, we had to pass through the mud and crush at the river-side, before we could take our boat, and Southward Ho! Now all can ride quietly with litter, coach, or mule, who are too exalted to walk as we are doing. It is nearly three o'clock, and we are at the doors. Now we hear the London cries to perfection. Tobacco and fruits, pamphlets and play-books, can be bought here. But no book of the play now performed—that will be published perhaps in some three years' time. The name of it is, however, exposed in red letters on a large placard outside the theatre. We may go into the ground or pit for sixpence, into the rooms or boxes for one or two shillings, or hire a stool on the stage for a shilling extra. Let us do so, for though there is no danger here, as at the penny house, of being pelted with nuts and apples from the galleries, it will be worth the extra shilling to see Burbadge off the stage, unless indeed they want double pay for this special performance. Had I thought of it we would have brought our own stools. Let us then enter at the actors' door, pass through the tiring-room, lift the traverse curtain, and take our places. We see that in honour of the new piece mats are spread on the stage, instead of the usual rushes. But the pit on the other side the green curtain are impatient, and are throwing missiles at us. Just lift it up, and return one or two at the ringleader of the understanders. Now the locality of the scene is placarded on the tapestry that is hung round the stage, and Burbadge enters in black to speak the prologue to the tragedy.

The musicians are in the stage boxes—ten of them; the best 'consort' in London; mostly Italians in his majesty's service. The trumpet has sounded thrice; the main curtains are drawn aside, and Burbadge, laurel in hand, begins the prologue. Before the act we have time for reflection during the music. The first thing that strikes us, is the advance that the drama has made since the old days when usurer Henslow paid his poets £6 or £8 for a play. Our poets now get from £12 to £20, besides their benefit on the second day, and their prospective profit when they publish their piece at sixpence, or their 'works' in folio, as Jonson has done. Yet their profits are as nothing compared to those of shareholders and actors. See how rich the Burbadges and Shakespeare have become. Even revivals of old pieces refashioned in one or two of their acts, bring in the money rapidly. The mere fees to the Master of the Revels produce him a handsome income. Next we are struck by the audience below us in the 'ground,' above us in the boxes, and around us on the stage; the eating nuts and russet pippins, the drinking canary and claret, the smoking pudding tobacco, the playing at primero and gleek and ruff. Even the city dames smoke, but they are masqued; yet there are unmasked women here too, but they cannot be of a high class. Notice their dress, their large ruffs, Venice chains, pomander necklaces, feather fans. On the stage itself, what with the gentry on the floor, who have no stools, their pages filling their pipes, and their frequent change of place, the actors have scarce room for their performance. The balcony at the back of the theatre where they enter 'above,' is, however, free from such intrusion, but it needs a stretch of imagination to conceive it, now as a mountain, now as a city wall, now as a chamber window. It serves

also for the playing of interludes or plays within plays.
The traverse under it is used for concealing beds to be drawn
out, dead bodies when lugged in, and the like. But the
groundlings are again impatient. They seem like to riot,
climb the stage, and drive out the actors. They have done
this ere now. But Burbadge comes forward and apologises:
'Bonduca's daughter is not shaved yet; wait a moment,
gentlemen, and she will appear.' This comes of the puritans
and their opposition to women-actors. But the bookholder
enters. Trumpets, hautboys, cornets, viols, and recorders,
have played their solemn dump, and the tragedy begins.
Notice the actors' grand dresses. They frequently cost five
times as much as the play itself. See in the ground the
critics, the coney catchers, the shorthand writers, busily at
work. If the booksellers try to publish an unauthorised copy
of this play, they will have the wrong sow by the ear.
Fletcher will get its issue stayed; he will not let his plays be
staled by the press, as Shakespeare used to, or as he himself did in Beaumont's time. Picking of teeth, swearing of
oaths, burning of juniper on all sides. The latter is welcome,
for the smells were becoming unbearable. Displaying of
humours, chattering a medley of language-scraps stolen
from abroad, discussions on Caranza and the duello, lessons
on the whiff, the Cuban ebullition, and other ways of
drinking tobacco, criticisms on the shapes of beards, and
the Italian custom of forks, the last news of Coryat, the
best way to handle your pocket looking-glass—these and the
like occupy the minds and tongues of the gallants between
the acts. But there is now only the play left to see, and we
came to-day, not to see that, but the seers of it, and the
actors of it, and their surroundings. We have seen of these
things all that our time will let us. The shadow-dance is
done; the puppets have melted and resolved into thin air.
We will draw the curtain here and retire each on our own
road; may the time we have spent together be the cause of
gentle dreams and pleasant reveries. And so, good night.

DOCUMENTARY APPENDIX.

I GIVE here various documents and lists which would have unduly interrupted the narratives if inserted in the body of the book.

I.—ABSTRACT OF SHAKESPEARE'S WILL, 25TH MARCH 1616.

The bequests are these:
1. To Judith Quiney (his daughter):
    a. £100 for marriage portion, to be paid within one year from Shakespeare's death. Interest till paid at 10 per cent.
    b. £50 on her surrendering Rowington Manor to Susanna Hall.
    c. £150 (life interest) if she be alive at the end of three years from date of will. To pass at her death to her children, or assigns if there be no children. If she die within the three years,
    £100 to be given to 'my niece' (grand-daughter), Elizabeth Hall.
    £50 to be given to Joan Hart (his sister) in life interest; afterwards to be equally divided among her children.
    The husband of Judith Quiney to have the use of the whole £150 if he assign his wife security in land.
    d. 'My broad silver and gilt bowl.'
2. To Joan Hart (his sister):
    a. 'All my wearing apparel.'
    b. Life interest in the house she occupies in Stratford, at rent of 12d. yearly.
3. To the three sons of Joan Hart—William, [Thomas,] and Michael—£5 each.
4. To Elizabeth Hall, 'my niece :'
    'All my plate except my broad silver and gilt bowl.'
5. To the poor of Stratford, £10.
6. To Thomas Combe, 'my sword.'
7. To Thomas Russel, £5.
8. To Francis Collins of Warwick, £13, 6s. 8d.

9. To William Walker, 'my godson,' £1.
10. To Hamlet Sadler, William Reynolds, Antony Nash, and to 'my fellows,' John Hemynge, Richard Burbage, and Henry Cundell, £1, 6s. 8d. each, to buy them rings.
11. To Susanna Hall (his daughter):
    a. The New Place and two other tenements in Henley Street, Stratford.
    b. All lands and tenements in Stratford-upon-Avon, Old Stratford, Bishopton, and Wilcombe.
    c. The tenement in Blackfriars, London, occupied by John Robinson.
    All these were entailed to the 'heirs-male' of Susanna Hall.
12. To 'my wife, my second best bed with the furniture.'
13. Remainder to John Hall (his son-in-law), and his daughter, Susanna Hall.

Witnesses.—Francis Collyns, Julius Shaw, John Robinson, Hamnet Sadler, Robert Whatcoat.

Overseers (executors).—Thomas Russel, Francis Collins.

II.—THE FAMILY OF SHAKESPEARE.

A. *Children of Richard Shakespeare, married to Margaret ——* (*buried 9th February* 1597).

Name.	Baptized.	Buried.
John.	? 1530.	1601. September 8.
Henry.		1596. December 29.

B. *Children of John Shakespeare, married, c.* 1557, *to Mary Arden* (*baptized c.* 1539, *buried 9th September* 1608).

Name.	Baptized.	Buried.
Joan.	1558. September 15.	? In infancy.
Margaret.	1562. December 2.	1563. April 30.
William.	1564. April 26.	1616. April 25.
Gilbert.	1566. October 13.	1612, at latest.
Joan.	1569. April 15.	1646. November 4.
Anne.	1571. September 28.	1579. April 4.
Richard.	1574. March 11.	1613. February 4.
Edmund.	1580. May 3.	1607. December 31.

C. *Children of William Shakespeare, married,* 28*th November* 1582, *Anne Hathaway.*

Name.	Baptized.	Buried.
Susanna.	1583. May 26.	1649. July 16.
Hamnet. } Judith. }	1585. February 2.	{ 1596. August 11. { 1662. February 9.

INTRODUCTION TO SHAKESPEARIAN STUDY. 77

D. (?) *Children of Richard Hathaway*, *married to* —— ——.

Name.	Baptized.	Buried.
Anne.	1556.	1623. August 8.
Johanna.	1566. May 6.	
Thomas.	1569. April 12.	
John.	1574. February 3.	
William.	1578. November 30.	

E. *Children of William Hart* (*buried* 17*th April* 1616), *married, c.* 1599, *to Joan Shakespeare.*

Name.	Baptized.	Buried.
William.	1600. August 28.	1639. March 29.
Mary.	1603. June 5.	1607. December 17.
Thomas.	1605. July 24.	
Michael.	1608. September 23.	

F. *Child of John Hall* (*buried 26th November* 1635), *married, 5th June* 1607, *to Susanna Shakespeare.*

Elizabeth (baptized 21st February 1608, buried February 1670), married (1) Thomas Nash, 22d April 1626; (2) Sir John Barnard. She left no issue. Thomas Nash (baptized 20th June 1593, buried 5th April 1647), was son of Antony Nash, buried 18th November 1622.

G. *Children of Richard Quiney* (*buried* 31*st May* 1602), *married to* —— ——.

Name.	Baptized.	Buried.
Adrian.	1586.	
Richard.	1587.	
Thomas.	1589. February 26.	? 1663.
William.	1593.	
John.	1597.	
George.	1600. April 9.	1624. April 11.

H. *Children of Thomas Quiney* (*baptized 26th February* 1589), *married,* 10*th February* 1616, *to Judith Shakespeare.*

Name.	Baptized.	Buried.
Shakespeare.	1616. November 23.	1617. May 8.
Richard.	1618. February 9.	1639. February 26.
Thomas.	1619. August 29.	1639. January 28.

There was a John Shakespeare in Stratford who married a Margery Roberts, 25th November 1584. She was buried 29th October 1587. He had issue by a second wife, Ursula, baptized 11th March 1589; Humphrey, 24th May 1590; Philip, 21st September 1591.

III.—ENTRIES AT STATIONERS' HALL.

Date.	Entered by	Name of Play, etc.
1592. Apr. 3.	Edw. White.	Arden of Feversham.
1593. Apr. 18.	Rich. Feild.	Venus and Adonis.
1594. Feb. 6.	John Danter.	Titus Andronicus.
,, Mar. 12.	Tho. Millington.	First Part of The Contention, etc.
,, May 2.	Peter Short.	Taming of a Shrew.
,, May 9.	Harrison Senr.	Ravishment of Lucrece.
,, May 14.	Tho. Creede.	Famous Victories of Hen. V.
,, May 14.	Edw. White.	Chronicle of Leir.
,, June 19.	Tho. Creede.	Rich. III (with Shore's Wife).
,, July 20.	Tho. Creede.	Locrine.
1595. Dec. 1.	Cuthbert Burby.	Edward III.
1596. June 3.	W. Leake.	Venus and Adonis.
,, Aug. 5.	Edw. White.	Romeo and Juliet.
,, Aug. 27.	*Tho. Millington.	Macdobeth. Taming of a Shrew.
1597. Aug. 15.	Rich. Jones.	Widow of Watling Street, Parts 1 and 2.
,, Aug. 29.	Andrew Wise.	Richard II.
,, Oct. 20.	Andrew Wise.	Richard III.
1598. Feb. 25.	Andrew Wise.	1 Henry IV.
,, July 22.	†James Roberts.	Merchant (or Jew) of Venice.
?1600. Aug. 4.	To be stayed.	Henry V. Every Man in his Humour. Much Ado about Nothing.
1600. Aug. 11.	Tho. Pavier.	History of Henry V.
,, Aug. 23.	And. Wise. Wm. Aspley.	Much Ado about Nothing. 2 Hen. IV, by Shakespeare.
,, Oct. 8.	Tho. Fisher.	Midsummer Night's Dream.
,, Oct. 28.	Tho. Haies.	Merchant of Venice.
1602. Jan. 18.	John Busby; assigned to Ar. Johnson.	Sir John Falstaff and the Merry Wives of Windsor.
,, Apr. 19.	Tho. Pavier; assigned from Tho. Millington, *salvo jure cujuscumque.*	1 Henry VI. 2 Henry VI.
,, Apr. 19.	Tho. Pavier.	Titus Andronicus.
,, July 26.	James Roberts.	Hamlet (Chamberlain's).
,, Aug. 11.	Wm. Cotton.	L. Cromwell (Chamberlain's).
1603. Feb. 7.	[James] Roberts.	Troilus and Cressida (Chamberlain's).
,, June 27.	Matt. Law.	Richard III. Richard II. 1 Henry IV. } All King's.

* Fined 2s. 6d. for printing a ballad contrary to order.
† Licence to be first had of the Lord Chamberlain.

Date.	Entered by	Name of Play, etc.
1605. May 8.	*Simon Stafford; assigned to John Wright.	King Leir (as lately acted).
,, July 3.	Tho. Pavyer.	Murther in Yorkshire (ballad).
1606. Jan. 22.	[Nich.] Ling.	Romeo and Juliet. Love's Labour Lost. Taming of a Shrew.
1607. Aug. 6.	Geo. Elde.	Puritan Widow.
,, Oct. 22.	Arth. Johnson.	Merry Devil of Edmonton.
,, Nov. 19.	John Smythick.	Hamlet. Taming of a Shrew. Romeo and Juliett. Love's Labour Lost.
,, Nov. 26.	Nath. Butter. John Busby.	Shakespeare's King Lear. (Played by King's servants of the Globe before James I, on St Stephen's night, 1606.)
1608. Apr. 5.	Joseph Hunt. Tho. Archer.	Merry Devil of Edmonton, by T. B.
,, May 2.	[Tho.] Pavyer.	Yorkshire Tragedy, by W. Shakespeare.
,, May 20.	Edw. Blount.	Pericles. Anthony and Cleopatra.
1609. Jan. 28.	Richard Bonion. Henry Whalley.	Troylus and Cressida.
,, May 20.	Tho. Thorpe.	Shakespeare's Sonnetts.
,, Oct. 16.	—— Welby.	Edward III.
1611. Dec. 16.	John Brown.	Lord Cromwell, by W. S.
1616. Feb. 16.	W. Barrett.	Venus and Adonis. Lord Cromwell.
1617. Mar. 2.	—— Snodham.	Edward III.
1618. Sep. 17.	John Wright.	Mucedorus.
1619. Mar. 8.	John Parker.	Venus and Adonis.
,, July 8.	Lau. Hayes.	Merchant of Venice.
1621. Oct. 6.	Thomas Walkely.	Othello.
1623. Nov. 8.	—— Blount. Isaac Jaggard.	Mr William Shakespeare's Comedies, Histories, and Tragedies, so many of the said copies as are not formerly entered to other men: *Comedies.* Tempest. Two Gentlemen of Verona. Measure for Measure.

* But Simon Stafford to have the printing of the book.

Date.	Entered by	Name of Play, etc.
		Comedies—continued.
		As You Like It.
		All's Well that Ends Well.
		Twelfth Night.
		Winter's Tale.
		Histories.
1623. Nov. 8.	—— Blount. / Isaac Jaggard.	3 Henry VI. / Henry VIII.
		Tragedies.
		Coriolanus.
		Timon of Athens.
		Julius Cæsar.
		Macbeth.
		Anthonie and Cleopatra.
		Cymbeline.
1624. Dec. 4.	[Tho.] Pavier.	Titus Andronicus. / Widow of Watling Street.
1625. Feb. 23.	—— Stansby.	Edward III.
1626. Apr. 3.	—— Parker.	Lord Cromwell.
		Mr Pavier's right in Shakespeare's plays, or any of them.
1626. Aug. 4.	Edw. Brewster. / Robt. Birde.	History of Henry V. / Play of the same.
		Sir John Oldcastle.
		Titus Andronicus.
		Hamlet.
1629. Jan. 29.	—— Meighen.	Merry Wives of Windsor.
		Henry V.
		Sir John Oldcastle.
		Tytus Andronicus.
1630. Nov. 3.	Ric. Cotes.	Yorke and Lancaster.
		Agincourt.
		Pericles.
		Hamblet.
		Yorkshire Tragedy.
1630. June 26.	Tho. Blount; assigned to Edw. Allott.	The sixteen plays mentioned under date 1623.

IV.—LIST OF QUARTO EDITIONS.

In the following list an asterisk (*) prefixed indicates that Shakespeare's name does not appear on the title-page. The order is nearly that of first publication.

Edward III.

No. of Quarto.	Date of Publication.	Printer.	Publisher.
Q. 1.	1596	——	Cuth. Burby.
Q. 2.	1599	S. Stafford.	Cuth. Burby.
Q. 3.	1609	——	—— Welby.
Q. 4.	1617	——	—— Snodham.
Q. 5.	1625	——	—— Stansby.

Venus and Adonis.

*Q. 1, *Q. 2.	1593-4	Rich. Field.	Rich. Field.
*Q. 3.	1596	R. F[ield].	J. Harrison.
*Q. 4.	1600	J. H[arrison].	J. Harrison.
*Q. 5.	1600	J. H[arrison].	J. Harrison.
*Q. 6, *Q. 7.	1602	——	W. Leake.
*Q. 8.	1617	——	W. B[arret].
*Q. 9.	1620	——	J. P[arker].
*Q. 10.	1627	Jno. Wreittoun.	——
*Q. 11?	1630	J. Wreittoun.	——
*Q. 12.	1630	J. H.	Francis Coles.
*Q. 13.	1636	J. H.	Francis Coles.

Lucrece.

*Q. 1.	1594	R. Field.	J. Harrison.
*Q. 2.	1598	P. S[hort].	J. Harrison.
*Q. 3.	1600	J. H[arrison].	J. Harrison.
*Q. 4.	1607	N. O[kes].	J. Harrison.
Q. 5.	1616	T. S.	Roger Jackson.
Q. 6	1624	J. B.	Roger Jackson.

Titus Andronicus.

*Q. 1.	1600	J. R[oberts].	Edw. White.
*Q. 2.	1611	——	Edw. White.

First Part of *The Contention.*

*Q. 1.	1594	Thos. Creed.	T. Millington.
*Q. 2.	1600	{ Val. Simmes. { W. W[aterson]. }	T. Millington.

Whole of *The Contention.*

Q. 3.	1619	——	T. P.

True Tragedy.

*Q. 1.	1595	P. S[hort].	T. Millington.
*Q. 2.	1600	W. W[aterson].	T. Millington.

Richard II.

*Q. 1.	1597	Val. Simmes.	And. Wise.
Q. 2.	1598	Val. Simmes.	And. Wise.
Q. 3 (+ IV, i, 154-318).	1608	W. W[aterson].	Mt. Law.
Q. 4.	1615	——	Mt. Law.
Q. 5.	1634	John Norton.	——

F

INTRODUCTION TO SHAKESPEARIAN STUDY.

Romeo and Juliet.

No. of Quarto.	Date of Publication.	Printer.	Publisher.
*Q. 1.	1597	John Danter.	
*Q. 2.	1599	Thos Creede.	Cuth. Burby.
Q. 3, Q. 4.	1609		John Smethwick.
Q. 5.	1637	R. Young.	John Smethwick(F)

Richard III.

*Q. 1.	1597	Val. Simmes.	And. Wise.
Q. 2.	1598	Tho. Creede.	And. Wise.
Q. 3.	1602	Tho. Creede.	And. Wise.
Q. 4.	1605	Tho. Creede.	Mt. Law.
Q. 5.	1612	Tho. Creede.	Mt. Law.
Q. 6.	1622	Tho. Purfoot.	Mt. Law.
Q. 7.	1629	Jno. Norton.	Mt. Law.
Q. 8.	1634	Jno. Norton.	

Love's Labour's Lost.

Q. 1.	1598	W. W[aterson].	Cuth. Burby.
Q. 2.	1631	W. S.	John Smethwicke.

1 Henry IV.

*Q. 1.	1598	P. S[hort].	A. Wise.
Q. 2.	1599	S. S[tafford].	A. Wise.
Q. 3.	1604	Val. Simmes.	Mt. Law.
Q. 4.	1608		Mt. Law.
Q. 5.	1613	W. W.	Mt. Law.
Q. 6.	1622	T. P[urfoot].	Mt. Law.
Q. 7.	1632	Jno. Norton.	Willm. Sheares.
Q. 8.	1639	Jno. Norton.	Hugh Perry.

Passionate Pilgrim.

Q. 1.	1599	Sold by W. Leake.	W. Jaggard (F.).
Q. 2.	1612		W. Jaggard.

Midsummer Night's Dream.

Q. 1.	1600		Th. Fisher.
Q. 2.	1600		J. Roberts.

Merchant of Venice.

Q. 1.	1600	J. Roberts.	
Q. 2.	1600	J. R[oberts].	Th. Heyes.
Q. 3.	1637	W. P.	Lawrence Heyes.
Q. 4.	1652		Wm. Leake.

2 Henry IV.

Q. 1.	1600 (bis)	V. S.	And. Wise and W. Aspley (F.).

Henry V.

*Q. 1.	1600	Th. Creede.	Th. Millington and T. Busby.
*Q. 2	1602	Th. Creede.	Th. Pavier.
*Q. 3.	1608		T. P[avier].

Much Ado about Nothing.

No. of Quarto.	Date of Publication.	Printer.	Publisher.
Q. 1.	1600	V. S.	And. Wise and Wm. Aspley.

Merry Wives of Windsor.

Q. 1.	1602	T. C[reede].	Art. Johnson.
Q. 2.	1619	———	Art. Johnson.
Q. 3.	1630	T. H.	R. Meighen.

Hamlet.

Q. 1.	1603	———	N. L[ing] and Jas. Trundell.
Q. 2, Q. 3.	1604-5	J. R[oberts].	N. L[ing].
Q. 4.	1611	———	John Smethwicke.
Q. 5.	———	W. S.	John Smethwicke.
Q. 6.	1637	R. Young.	John Smethwicke.

King Lear.

Q. 1.	1608	———	Nath. Butter.
Q. 2.	1608	———	Nath. Butter.

Sonnets.

Sold by W. Aspley.	1609	G. Eld.	T. T[horpe].
Sold by J. Wright.	1609	G. Eld.	T. T[horpe].

Troilus and Cressida.

Q. 1.	1609 (*bis*)	G. Eld.	R. Bonian and H. Whalley.

Pericles.

Q. 1, Q. 2.	1609 (*bis*)	———	H. Gosson.
Q. 3.	1611	S. S[tafford].	———
Q. 4.	1619	———	T. P[avier].
Q. 5.	1630	J. N[orton].	R. B[ird].
Q. 6.	1635	Th. Cotes.	———

Othello.

Q. 1.	1622	N. O[kes].	Th. Walkley.
Q. 2.	1630	A. M.	Rd. Hawkins.
Q. 3.	1655	———	Wm. Leake.

Two Noble Kinsmen.

Q. 1.	1634	T. Cotes.	J. Waterson.

V.—EXTRACTS FROM THE ACCOUNTS OF THE REVELS AT COURT.

These are very important for early stage history, and contain mention of various plays on which Shakespeare probably founded some of his.

A. CHILDREN'S COMPANIES.

MERCHANT TAYLORS'.	WESTMINSTER.	WINDSOR.	CHAPEL.	PAUL'S.
Richard Muncaster, *Manager*.	John Taylor, *Manager*.	Richard Farrant, *Manager*.	Richard Bowyer, *Manager*.	Sebastian Westcott, *Manager*.
....	Paris and Vienna (Shrove Tuesday) William Elderton, *Manager*.	Ajax and Ulysses (New Year).	Narcisse (Twelfth Day). John Honnis, *Manager*.	Efiginia (Innocents' Day).
....	Unknown Play (Shrove Tuesday). Truth, Ffaithfulnesse, and Mercy (New Year's Day).	Unknown Play (St John's Day). Quint Ffabi (Twelfth Day).	Unknown Play (Twelfth Day).	Unknown Play (New Year). Alkmeon. (St John's).
Timoclia (Candlemas). Percius and Anthomiris (Shrove Tuesday).	....	....	....	....
Unknown Play (Shrove Sunday).	....	Unknown Play (St John's). Mutius Sceuola (Twelfth Day).	....	Unknown Play (Twelfth Day). Historie of Error (New Year). Titus and Gisippus (Shrove Tuesday).
....	....	Unknown Play (Shrove Monday).	William Hunnis, *Manager*.	
....	....	....	Unknown Play (St John's).	Marryage of Mynde and Measure (Sun. after N. Year).

INTRODUCTION TO SHAKESPEARIAN STUDY. 85

		EARL OXFORD'S.		
1579-80.	....		Loyalty and Beauty (Shrove Monday).	Cipio African (Sun. after N. Year).
1580-1.	....	....	Alucius (St John's).	Pompey (Twelfth Night).
1581-2.	Ariodante & Geneuora (Shrove Tuesday).	Agamemnon & Ulisses (St John's).	Unknown Play (Shrove Sunday). Game of the Cards (St Stephen's).	....
1582-3.	....	....	Unknown Play (December 31).	Pompey (St Stephen's). **Thomas Giles,** *Manager.*
1588.	....	....	Unknown Play (Shrove Tuesday).	Unknown Play (Shrove Sunday).
1588-9.	....	....	....	Unknown Plays (Three days).
1589-90.	....	....	....	Unknown Play (Sun. after Xmas.). Unknown Play (New Year's Day). Unknown Play (Twelfth Day). **Edward Piers,** *Manager.*
1601.	....		....	Unknown Play (New Year's Day).

Lyly's plays were also performed by the Paul's Children 1584-9 (unfortunately the entries are lost): *Campaspe* on Twelfth Day 1583-4; *Sapho and Phao*, Shrove Tuesday 1583-4; *Endymion*, Candlemas 158-; *Gallathea*, New Year's Day 158-; *Midas*, Twelfth Day 158-; *Love's Metamorphosis*, 158-; *Woman in the Moon*, before 1584; *Mother Bombie*, 158-.
ˣ In this year were played [*Theagines and*] *Cariclea*, and *Fortune*.

B. MEN'S COMPANIES.

Sir R. Lane's.	R. Dudley, Earl Leicester's.	Fynes, Lord Clinton's, d. 1585.	Ratcliff, Earl Sussex's, died 1583.
Laurence Dutton, *Manager*.	James Burbadge, John Parkyn, John Lanham, William Johnson, Robert Wilson, *Managers*.	....	....
Lady Barbara (St John's). Cloridon & Radiamanta (Shrove Sunday). Two unknown Plays (St Stephen's Day and Shrove Sunday).	....	....	(Chamberlain, 1572.)
J. Dudley, Earl Warwick's.	Predor and Lucia (St Stephen's). Mamillia (Innocents' Day). Philemon and Philecia (Shrove Monday). Panecia (Candlemas).*	Herpetulus the Blew Knighte, and Perobia (3d January, Sunday).	....
Laurence Dutton and John Dutton, *Managers*.	....	Pretestus.	Phidrastus (Candlemas).* Phigon and Lucia. Unknown Play (Candlemas).
Three unknown Plays (St Stephen's Day, New Year's Day, &	Unknown Play (Candlemas).	Lord P. Howard, Earl Arundel's.	

INTRODUCTION TO SHAKESPEARIAN STUDY.

			Stanley, EARL DERBY'S, died 1593.	**Cary,** LORD HUNSDON'S.
1578-9.	Three Systers of Mantua (St Stephen's). Unknown Play (prepared, not shown, Candlemas). Knight in Burnyng Rock (Shrove Sunday).	Greeke Maide (Sunday after New Year). Rape of Second Helene (Twelfth Day).	....	Creweltie of a Stepmother (Innocents' Day). Murderous Michael (Shrove Tuesday).
1579-80.	Foure Sonnes of Fabyous (New Year's Day).	Unknown Play (prepared, not shown—Innocents' Day). Unknown Play (Twelfth Night).	Soldan and Duke of —— (Shrove Sunday).	Duke of Millayn and Marques of Mantua (St Stephen's). Portio and Demorantes (Candlemas). Serpedon (Shrove Tuesday).
1580-1. 1581-2.	....	Delight (St Stephen's). Unknown Play (Shr. Tues.). Telomo (Shrove Sunday).	Unknown Play (N.Y. Day). Love and Fortune (Sun. before New Year).	Unknown Play (St John's). Unknown Play (Candl.). Ferrar (Twelfth Day).
1582-3.	....	....	....	
	Queen's.			
1584-5. " " " "	Phillyda and Choryn (St Stephen's). Felix and Philiomena (Sunday after New Year). Fyve Plays in One (Twelfth Day). Three Plays in One (not shown, prepared for Shrove S). Antick Play and Comedy (Shrove Tuesday).		....	Bewtie and Huswyfery (St John's Day). ....

* There is some mistake here. Masks are not noticed in these tables.
† *Cutwell* was another play performed this year.
‡ Paid to the Lord Chamberlain's players. —CHALMERS.

VI.—EXTRACTS FROM HENSLOW'S 'DIARY,' GIVING LIST OF PLAYS PERFORMED AT THE ROSE THEATRE, 1592-7.

Lord Strange's Men.

Date.			Name of Play.		No. of Representations.
1591-2.	Feb.	19.	*Friar Bacon* (Saturday),		4
,,	,,	20.	*Mulomorco* [Battle of Alcazar],		11
,	,,	21.	*Orlando*,		1
,,	,,	23.	*Spanish Comedy, Don Horatio* [Jeronimo],		3
,,	,,	24.	Sir John Mandeville,		5
,,	,,	25.	Harry of Cornwall,		3
,,	,,	26.	*Jew of Malta*,		10
,,	,,	28.	Clorys and Orgasto,		1
?	Mar.	1.	Pope Joan,		1
,,	,,	2.	Machiavel,		3
,,	,,	3.	*Henry VI* [Part 1],	new	13
,,	,,	4.	Bendo and Ricardo,		3
,,	,,	6.	Four Plays in One,		4
,,	,,	8.	*Looking Glass*,		4
,,	,,	9.	Zenobia,		1
,,	,,	14.	*Jeronimo* [Spanish Tragedy],		14
,,	,,	21.	Constantine,		1
,,	,,	22.	Jerusalem,		2
,,	Apr.	6.	Brandymer,		2
,,	,,	10.	*Comedy of Jeronymo*,		4
,,	,,	11.	Titus and Vespasia[n],*	new	7
1592.	,,	28.	Tambercam (Second Part),	new	5
,,	May	14.	Harry V,		7
,,	,,	23.	Tanner of Denmark,	new	1
,,	June	[10].	Knack to Know a Knave,	new	3
,,	Jan.	5.	Gelyous Comedy,	new	1
1592-3.	,,	12.	Cosmo, ,,		2
,,	,,	30.	*Tragedy of the Guise*,	new	1

Earl of Sussex's Men, beginning 27th December.

1593.	Dec.	27.	God speed the Plough,		2
,,	,,	28.	Hewen of Burdoche (Huon of Bordeaux),		3
,,	,,	29.	George a Green,		4
,,	,,	30.	Buckingham,		4
,,	,,	31.	Richard the Confessor,		2
1593-4.	Jan.	4.	William the Conqueror,		1
,,	,,	7.	Friar Francis,		3
,,	,,	8.	*Pinner of Wakefield* (George a Green),		1
,,	,,	9.	Abram and Lot,		3
,,	,,	12.	Fair Maid of Italy,		2
,,	,,	18.	King Lud,		1
,,	,,	23.	*Titus and Andronicus*,	new	3

* Exists in a German version.

INTRODUCTION TO SHAKESPEARIAN STUDY. 89

Date.			Name of Play.		No. of Representations.
Queen's and Lord Sussex's, beginning at Easter.					
1594?	Apr.	2.	Ranger's Comedy,		1
,,	,,	6.	King Lear,		2
Lord Admiral's Men, beginning 14th May.					
1594.	May	16.	Cutlack,		1
Lord Admiral's and Lord Chamberlain's, beginning at Newington.					
,,	June	3.	Hester and Ahasuerus,		2
,,	,,	4.	*Jew of Malta,*		18
,,	,,	5.	*Andronicus,*		2
,,	,,	6.	Cutlack,		12
,,	,,	8.	Bellendon,	new	17
,,	,,	9.	Hamlet,		1
,,	,,	11.	*Taming of a Shrew,*		1
,,	,,	18.	Ranger's Comedy,		10
,,	,,	19.	*Guise,*		10
,,	,,	26.	Galiaso,	new	9
,,	July	9.	Philippo and Hippolito,		12
,,	,,	19.	Godfrey of Boulogne (Second Part),*	new	11
,,	,,	30.	Merchant of Emden,	new	1
,,	Aug.	11.	Tasso's Melancholy,	new	13
,,	,,	14.	Mahomet,		8
,,	,,	25.	Venetian Comedy,	new	11
,,	,,	28.	*Tamberlane,*		23
,,	Sept.	17.	Palamon and Arsett,	new	4
,,	,,	24.	Venetian, and Love of an English Lady,	new	1
,,	,,	30.	*Doctor Faustus,*		24
,,	Oct.	4.	Love of a Grecian Lady,		12
,,	,,	18.	French Doctor,		11
,,	,,	22.	*Knack to Know an Honest* [*Man*],	new	19
,,	Nov.	8.	Cæsar and Pompey,	new	8
,,	,,	16.	Dioclesian,		2
,,	,,	30.	Warlam Chester,		7
,,	Dec.	2.	Wise Man of Chester,	new	20
,,	,,	14.	Set at Mawe,	new	4
,,	,,	19.	*Tamberlane* (*Second Part*),		11
,,	,,	26.	Siege of London,		12
,,	Jan.	4.	Velya,		—
1594-5.	Feb.	11.	French Comedy,	new	6
,,	,,	14.	Long Meg of Westminster,		18
,,	,,	21.	The Macke,	new	1
,,	Mar.	5.	Steleo (Celio) and Olempo,	new	7
1595.	May	7.	Herculous (First Part),	new	10
,,	,,	18.	Galfrido and Bernardo,		—
,,	,,	23.	Herculous (Second Part),	new	8

* Probably same as *The Four Prentises of London.*

90 INTRODUCTION TO SHAKESPEARIAN STUDY.

Date.			Name of Play.		No. of Represen-tations.
1595.	June	3.	Seven Days of the Week,	*new*	19
,,	,,	18.	Cæsar (Second Part),	*new*	2
,,	,,	20.	Antonye and Vallea,	.	3
,,	Aug.	29.	Longshank,	*new*	14
,,	Sept.	4.	Olimpeo and Hengenyo,	.	—
,,	,,	5.	Crack me this Nut,	*new*	16
,,	,,	17.	(New) World's Tragedy,	*new*	11
,,	Oct.	2.	Disguises,	*new*	6
,,	,,	15.	Wonder of a Woman,	*new*	10
,,	,,	28.	Bernardo and Fiametta,	*new*	7
,,	Nov.	14.	Toy to Please my Lady (Chaste Ladies),	*new*	7
,,	,,	28.	*Harry V* [*Famous Victories of*],	*new*	13
,,	,,	29.	Welshman,	.	1
1595-6.	Jan.	3.	Chinon of England,	*new*	11
,,	,,	16.	Pythagoras,	*new*	13
,,	,,	22.	Second Week,	*new*	2
,,	Feb.	3.	*Fortunatus* (First Part),	.	7
,,	,,	12.	*Blind Beggar of Alexandria*,	*new*	13
1596.	Apr.	29.	Julian Apostata,	*new*	3
,,	May	6.	Tambercam,	*new*	—
,,	,,	19.	Phocas,	*new*	7
,,	June	11.	Tambercam (Second Part),	*new*	—
,,	,,	23.	Troy [? Heywood's *Iron Age*],	*new*	4
,,	July	1.	Paradox,	*new*	1
,,	,,	18.	Tinker of Totness,	*new*	—

Lord Admiral's, beginning Simon and Jude's Day (Oct. 28).
Lord Admiral's, beginning 25th November.

,,	Dec.	4.	Valtiger,	*new*	12
,,	,,	11.	*Stewtley*,	*new*	11
,,	,,	19.	Nebuchadonizer,	*new*	8
,,	,,	30.	That will be shall be,	*new*	12
1596-7.	Jan.	14.	Alexander and Lodowick,	*new*	15
,,	,,	27.	Woman Hard to Please,	*new*	12
,,	Feb.	3.	Osric,	.	2
,,	Mar.	19.	Guido,	*new*	5
,,	Apr.	7.	Five Plays in One,	*new*	10
1597.	,,	13.	Time's Triumph and Faustus,	.	1
,,	,,	18.	French Comedy,	*new*	—
,,	,,	29.	Uter Pendragon,	*new*	5
,,	May	11.	Comedy of Humours,	*new*	11
,,	,,	26.	Harry I, Life and Death,	*new*	6
,,	June	3.	Frederycke and Basellia (Basilea),*	*new*	4
,,	,,	22.	Henges,	.	1
,,	,,	30.	Life and Death of Martin Swart,	*new*	3
,,	July	14.	Witch of Islington,	.	2

* The plot of the play is extant.

INTRODUCTION TO SHAKESPEARIAN STUDY. 91

Date.   Name of Play.
Lord Admiral's and Lord Pembroke's, beginning 11th October.
1597. Oct. 11. Jeronymo.
  „   „   —   Comedy of Humours [*Humorous Day's Mirth*].
  „   „   —   Doctor Faustus.
  „   „   19. Hardacute [Hardicanute].
  „   „   31. Friar Spendleton.
  „   Nov.   2. Bourbon.
  „   „   3. Knewtus.
  „   „   4. Umers.

The number of representations is taken from Malone. He is responsible for the counting.

Books belonging to stock, and such as I have bought since 3d March 1598.

Black Joan.
Humours.
Hardacanute.
Bourbonne.
Sturg flattery.
Brunhowlle.
Cobler of Queenhithe.
Friar Pendleton.
Alice Pierce.
Red Cap.
Robin Hood, 1.
  „   2.
Phaeton.
Treangel [Triangle of] Cuckolds.

Goodwin [1].
Woman will have her Will.
Welshman's Price.
King Arthur, Life and Death.
Hercules, 1.
  „   2.
Pythagoras.
Phocas.
Alexander and Lodowick.
Black Batman, 1.
  „   „   2.
Goodwin, 2.
Madman's Morris.
Pierce of Winchester.
Vayvode.

Pembroke's, beginning 18th October 1600.
1600. Oct. 28. Like unto Like.
  „   „   29. Roderick.

The plays printed in italics are still extant.

VII.—HENSLOW'S 'DIARY' CONTINUED, 1597-1604.

The following list is the most important of all the documents connected with the early drama. It is condensed from Henslow's *Diary*, and has never been tabulated till now. In the first and second columns, I give the month and day of the earliest and latest entries of payment to the writers; in the third, the name of the play; in the fourth, the names of the authors abbreviated, with the separate payments made by Henslow to each; in the fifth, the total payments; in the sixth, *f.* (full) indicates that the play was completed; *n.* (new) that the play was begun; and *o.* (old) that the play was revived; in the seventh I give the money laid out on dresses, etc.

ADMIRAL'S PLAYERS, 11TH OCTOBER 1597 TO 18TH JULY 1598.

First Date.	Last Date.	Name of Play.	Writers' Names and Payments.	Total Payments.			New or Old Play.	Money laid out.		
				£	s.	d.		£	s.	d.
Oct. 21	...	Cobler [of Queenhithe],	Anon,	2	0	0	*o*			
Nov. 5	...	A Book [Woman willhave her will]	Hg,	0	10	0				
,, 26	...	Branhowlte,	Anon,		...		*o*	4	0	0
Dec. 8	Dec. 10	Alice Pierce,	Anon,		...		*o*	2	2	7
,, 3	...	A Book,	Jn,	1	0	0	*n*			
,, 22	Jan. 3	Mother Redcap,	Mn, Dr, 60s, 55s; Mn, 5s,	6	0	0	*f*			
Jan. 3	,, 8	Dido and Æneas,	Anon,		...		*o*	2	19	0
,, 8	...	A Book [*Phaeton*],	Dk,	1	0	0	*n*			
,, 15	...	*Phaeton* [*Sun's Darling*],	Dk,	4	0	0	*n*	3	0	0
Feb. 15	...	1 *Robin Hood*,	Mn,	5	0	0	*n*			
,, 18	May 2-6	Woman will have her Will,	Hg, 20s, 20s,	2	0	0	*n*			
,, 20	Mar. 8	2 *Robin Hood* (Downfall of Earl Huntingdon),	Mn, 10s, 5s; Ct, 20s; [Mn, Ch,]60s,	4	15	0	*n*			
,, 22	...	Miller,	Anon,	1	0	0	*o*			
Mar. 1	...	Triplicity of Cuckolds,	Dk,	5	0	0	*n*			
,, 13	...	A Book, wherein is a part of a Welshman,	Dr, Ct,	2	0	0	*n*			
...	...	Famous Wars of Henry I, and the Prince of Wales,	Dr, Dk, Ct,	4	5	0	*j*	0	8	0
,, 25	Mar. 30	Godwin and his Three Sons,	Dr, Dk, Ct, Wl, 80s, 40s,	6	0	0	*f*	1	4	0
...	...	Piers of Exton,	Dr, Dk, Ct, Wl,	2	0	0	*n*			
Apr. 12	...	Life of King Arthur,	Ht,	4	0	0	*j*	3	0	0

				£ s. d.	
May 2-6		Black Batman of the North,	Ct, 20s; Wl, Dr, Dk, Ct, 120s,	7 0 0	f
Apr. 6 (May)	May 22 June 10	2 Godwin,	Ct, Dk, 20s; Dr, 10s, 30s; Wl, 10s; Ct, 10s,	4 0 0	f
May 16	May 23.	A Book [Will of a Woman],	Cp, 40s, 20s [? 10 June, 10s],	3 0 0	n
,, 16	Alex. & Lod. not delivered till July 18.	5 Books: 1, 2 Hercules; Phocas; Pythagoras; Alexander and Lodowick,	Sl, 140s, 20s,	8 0 0	o (Hercules)
May 30		Love prevented,	Pr,	4 0 0	n
June 13	June 26	Richard Cœur de Lion's Funeral,	Wl, 5s, 20s; Ct, 5s, 5s, 25s; Ct, Wl, Mn, 15s; Mn, 20s; Dr, 30s,	6 5 0	f
,, 15		Will of a Woman,*	Cp,	1 0 0	n
,, 26	July 14	2 Black Batman of the North,	Ct, 20s, 60s, 15s; Wl, 10s, 15s,	6 0 0	f
,, 31†	,, 10	Madman's Morris,	Wl, Dr, Dk, 60s; Dr, 20s; Wl, Dk, 40s,	6 0 0	f
July 14		Woman Tragedy,	Ct,	5 0 0	n
,, 17	Jul. 18 (28)	Hannibal and Hermes [Worse Feared than Hurt],	Wl, 10s, 20s; Wl, Dr, Dk, 60s; Dr, Dk, 30s, 10s,	6 10 0	f
,, 19		Valentine and Orson,	Ht, Mn,	5 0 0	f
Jul. 18 (28)	Aug. 10	Pierce of Winchester,	Dk, 10s; Dr, Wl, Dk, 50s, 50s,	6 0 0	f
				27 2 0	

ADMIRAL'S PLAYERS, 30TH JULY 1598 TO 16TH APRIL 1599.

				£ s. d.	
July 30	Oct. 22	Conquest of Brute, with the First Finding of the Bath,	Dy, 40s; Ct, 9s, 20s, 5s,	3 14 0†	} f
Aug. 9	...	Comedy for the Court,	Ct, 10s, 60s, 50s, Mn,	6 0 0 0 10 0	n
				4 4 0	

* Probably the same as *Monsieur d'Olive*.   † *Sic*.   ‡ This sum is probably included in the £6 in the next line.

ADMIRAL'S PLAYERS, 30TH JULY 1598 TO 16TH APRIL 1599—*Continued*.

First Date.	Last Date.	Name of Play.	Writers' Names and Payments.	Total Payments. £ s. d.	New or Old Play.	Money laid out. £ s. d.
Aug. 18	...	Hot Anger soon Cold,	Pr, Ct, Jn,	6 0 0	f	
,, 19	Aug. 24	Chance Medley,	Wl, 30s; Ct, 30s; Mn, 25s; Dr, 35s,	6 0 0	f	
,, 21	,, 29	Catiline,	Wl, 10s, 10s; Ch, 5s,	1 5 0	n	
,, 29	...	Vayvode (? old play altered),	Ct,	1 0 0	...	17 5 0
... 30	Jan. 21	Worse afeared than hurt (? 2d part),	Bought of Allen,	2 0 0	...	
,, 30	Aug. 4 (Sept.)		Dr, Dk, 50s, 50s,	5 0 0	f	
Sept. 29	...	1 Civil Wars in France,	Dr, Dk,	6 0 0	f	10 0 0
,, 31*	Oct. 12	Fountain of New Fashions,†	Cp, 60s, 20s,	4 0 0	f	17 0 0
Oct. 3	...	Mulmutius Dunwallow,	Rn,	3 0 0	o	
,, 16	,, 20	Connan, Prince of Cornwall,	Dr, Dk, 30s, 10s, 80s,	6 0 0	f	
,, 23	...	Mr Chapman's play book, and 2 acts of a tragedy of Benjamin [Jonson]'s plot,	Cp,	3 0 0	n	
Nov. 3	...	2 Civil Wars of France,	Dr, Dk,	6 0 0	f	20 0 0
,, 18	Dec. 30	3 Civil Wars of France,	Dr, Dk, 20s, 100s,	6 0 0	f	
,, 18	...	Mending 1 *Robin Hood*,	Ct,	0 10 0	o	
,, 25	Nov. 28	"Tis no Deceit to Deceive the Deceiver; for mending *Robin Hood* for the Court,	Ct, 10s, 20s,	1 10 0	n	
Dec. 6	Jan. 26	War without Blows, and Love without Suit (Strife),	Hy, 60s, 40s,	5 0 0	f	

INTRODUCTION TO SHAKESPEARIAN STUDY. 95

Date	Title	Notes	£	s	d	
Dec. 22	2 Two Angry Women of Abingdon,	Pr, 100s, 40s,	7	0	0	
Jan. 4	Three Acts of a Tragedy,	Cp, 60s, 60s,	6	0	0	ƒ 11 0 0
,, 20	William Longbeard,	Dr,	3	0	0	n
,, 20	First Introduction of the Civil Wars of France,	Dk,	3	0	0	n
Jan. 22	*World Runs on Wheels* (All Fools but the Fool),	Cp, 60s, 20s, 40s, 30s,	8	10	0	n
Feb. 10	Joan as Good as my Lady,	Hy, 60s, 40s,	5	0	0	ƒ
,, 10	Friar Fox and Julian of Brentford,	Anon,	5	10	0	n 0 8 0
,, 16	Troy's Revenge (with Tragedy of Polyphemus),	Ct, 20s, 100s (50s only in cash),	6	0	0	ƒ
,, 28	Two Merry Women of Abingdon,	Pr,	2	0	0	n
Mar. 4	Spencers,	Ct, 10s; Pr, 110s,	6	0	0	ƒ 30 0 0
...	Four Kings,	Licensed.				
...	Brute Greenshield,	Licensed.				
,, 31	Alexander and Lodowick,	....	...	0	0	o 5 0 0
April 7	Troilus and Cressida,	Dk, Ct, 60s, 20s,	4	0	0	n
,, 9	Placidas,	Ct,	0	10	0	n
May 2	Orestes Furies,	Dk,	0	5	0	n

ADMIRAL'S PLAYERS, 26TH MAY 1599 TO 10TH JULY 1600.

Date	Title	Notes	£	s	d	
May 26	Agamemnon,	Dk, Ct, 30s, 65s,	4	15	0	ƒ
May 30	Gentle Craft (*Shoemaker's Holiday*),	Dk,	3	0	0	o
July 15	Pastoral Tragedy,‡					
,, 17		Cp,	2	0	0	n

* Sic.   † Probably the same as *The Gentleman Usher*.   ‡ Query same as *May-day*.   Henslow often confuses tragedy and comedy.

ADMIRAL'S PLAYERS, 26TH MAY 1599 TO 10TH JULY 1600—Continued.

First Date.	Last Date.	Name of Play.	Writers' Names and Payments.	Total Payments. £ s. d.	New or Old Play.	Money laid out. £ s. d.
July 24	Oct. 14	Stepmother's Tragedy,	Dk, 10s; Dk, Ct, 20s; Ct, 20s, 80s,	6 10 0	f	
Aug. 1	...	Bear a Brain (Better Late than Never),	Dk, .	2 0 0	o	
,, 10	Sept. 2	Page of Plymouth,	Dk, Jn, 40s, 120s,	8 0 0	f	10 0 0
,, 20	,, 27	Poor Man's Paradise,	Hg, 13s, 17s,	1 10 0	n	
Sept. 3	,, 27	Robert II, King of Scots, Tragedy,	Jn, Dk, Ct, etc., 40s; Dk, Ct, 20s; Ct, 10s; Jn, 20s,	6 10 0	f	
,, 28	...	A Book,	Mr Mastone, the new poet,	2 0 0	n	
Oct. 13	...	Tristram de Lyons,	Anon,	3 0 0	o	
,, 16	...	1, 2, *Life of Sir John Oldcastle*,	Mn, Dr, Wl, Ht, 200s, 10s,	10 10 0	f	1 0 0
...	Dec. 29	*Patient Grissel*,	Ct, 20s; Dk, Ct, Hg, 60s, 120s;* Dk, 5s; Hg, 5s,	10 10 0	f	
Nov. 1	Nov. 14	John Cox of Collumpton,	Hg, 20s; Hg, Dy, 20s, 60s,	5 0 0	n	
,, 8	...	2 Henry Richmond,	Wl, .	8 0 0	f	10 0 0
,, 9	Nov. 30	*Whole History of Fortunatus*,	Dk, 40s, 60s, 20s,	6 0 0	f	
,, 10	...	A Book [Tragedy of Orphans],	Ct, .	0 10 0	n	
,, 21	Dec. 6	Tragedy of Merry (Beech's Trag.),	Hg, 10s; Dy, 10s; Hg, Dy, 20s, 20s, 40s,	5 0 0	n	
,, 27	{1601 Sep.24}	Tragedy of Orphans,	Ct, 10s, 10s,	1 0 0	o	
,, 31†	...	Altering *Fortunatus*,	Dk, .	1 0 0	o	10 0 0
Dec. 12	...	End of *Fortunatus* for the Court,	Dk, .	2 0 0	o	

INTRODUCTION TO SHAKESPEARIAN STUDY. 97

				£	s	d		£	s	d
Dec. 13	Dec. 17	Arcadian Virgin,	Ch, Hg, 10s, 5s,	0	15	0	*n*			
...	Jan. 10	2 Sir John Oldcastle,	Dr,	4	0	0	*n*			
...	...	Italian Tragedy,	Dy,	2	0	0	*n*	1	10	0
...	...	Owen Tudor,	Dr, Mn, Ht, Wl,	4	0	0	*n*			
...	Jan. 18	Truth's Supplication to Candle-light,	Dk, 20s, 20s,	2	0	0	*n*			
Feb. 9	Jan. 30	Jugurth,	By,	1	10	0	*n*			
,, 13	...	Spanish Moor's Tragedy,‡	Dk, Hg, Dy,	3	0	0	*n*			
,, 16	Apr. 27	Damon and Pythias,	Ct, 20s, 26s, 30s, 44s,	6	0	0	*f*			
Mar. 1	May 16						*f*	38	0	0
	Mar. 8	Seven Wise Masters,	Ch, Dk, Hg, Dy, 40s; Ch, Dy, 50s; Ch, 30s,	6	0	0	*n*			
,, 18	...	Ferrex and Porrex,	Hg, 20s, 5s, 7s, 63s,	4	15	0	*n*			
Apr. 16	Apr. 24	English Fugitives,	Hg, 10s, 20s,	1	10	0	*j*			
...	May 14	Golden Age (Cupid and Psyche),	Dk, Dy, 30s; Dk, Dy, Ct, 60s, 30s,	6	0	0	*n*	2	0	0
Mar. 6	...	Wooing of Death,	Ct,	1	0	0	*n*			
(May)	...	Devil and his Dame,§	Hg,	0	5	0	*f*			
May 17	...	Strange News out of Poland,	Hg, Pt,	6	0	0	*f*			
,, 26	...	Blind Beggar of Bethnal Green,	Ct, Dy,	5	10	0	*n*	3	0	0
,, 27	...	Indes [Indies or Judas?]	Hg,	0	10	0	*f*			
June 3	June 14	1 Fair Constance of Rome,	Dr, Ht, Mn, Dk, 65s, 44s,	5	9	0	*n*			
,, 19	...	A Book,	Ct, Dy,	0	10	0	*n*			
,, 20	...	2 Constance of Rome,	Ht,	1	0	0	*n*			

* This £6 probably includes the preceding payments.   † *Sic.*
‡ Probably the same as *Lust's Dominion; or, The Lascivious Queen.*   § *See* 7th September 1602 (Worcester's players), p. 102.

ADMIRAL'S PLAYERS, 14TH AUGUST 1600 TO 18TH JANUARY 1602.

First Date.	Last Date.	Name of Play.	Writers' Names and Payments.	Total Payments. £ s. d.	New or Old Play.	Money laid out. £ s. d.
Sept. 6	...	Forteion Tenes,	Dk, .	1 0 0	n	1 0 0
Dec. 14	Dec. 22	*Phaeton* (altered for Court),	Dk, 10s, 30s, .	2 0 0	o	
,, 20	Jan. 13	Robin Hood's Pen'orths,	Hg, 20s, 10s, 10s, 40s,	4 0 0	n	
Jan. 3	,, 12	Hannibal and Scipio,	Rn, Ht, 40s, 5s, 75s,	6 0 0	f	
,, 23	Mar. 8	Book wherein is Skogan and Skelton,	Rn, Ht, 10s, 30s, 20s, 40s, 18s; Rn, 2s,	6 0 0	f	1 10 0
,, 29	,, 10	2 Blind Beggar of Bethnal Green, with the end of Stroud,	Hg, Dy, 40s, 30s, 30s, 30s, 10s,	6 0 0	f	
Mar. 24	Apr. 16	Conquest of Spain, by John à Gaunt,	Rn, Ht, 10s, 5s, 20s, 4s, .	1 19 0	n	
,, 31	,, 6	All is not Gold that Glisters,	Ct, 40s, 80s, .	6 0 0	f	15 5 9
Apr. 4	Sept. 1	Conquest of the West Indies,*	Dy, Hg, 40s, 10s; Sm, Hg, 20s; Hg, 5s; Dy, 20s, 10s, 20s, 10s,	6 15 0	?	
,, 18	May 22	King Sebastian of Portugal,	Dk, Ct, 20s, 40s; Dk, 60s,	6 0 0	f	6 3 4
May 2	,, c. 23	*Blind Beggar of Alexandria*,	Revived, .	...	o	5 10 0
,, 19	...	*Jew of Malta*,	Revived, .	...	o	6 1 0
,, 20	June 8	Six Yeomen of the West,	Hg, 10s, 5s, 40s, 15s, 30s,	5 0 0	f	6 6 10
,, 21	July 30	3 Thomas Stroud,	Dy, 10s, 5s; Hg, 10s; Dy, Hg, 40s, 65s,	6 0 0	f	
June 5	Aug. 24	Cardinal Wolsey's Life,†	Ct, 20s, 20s, 40s, 20s, 20s,	6 0 0	f	38 17 8
,, 13	Jul. 23-5	Life of the Humorous Earl of Gloster, and his Conquest of Portugal,	Wd, 20s, 10s, .	1 10 0	n	

Date	Play	Notes	£	s	d
July 4	Friar Rush and the Proud Woman of Antwerp,	Dy, Hg, 20s, 30s; Hg, 10s, 20s, 20s,	5	0	f
,, 30	2 Thomas Dough,		4	0	n
Aug. 22	Mahomet,	Hg, Dy, 10s, 60s: Hg, 10s,	2	0	0	3	12	1
Sept. 19	Wiseman of Westchester,	Bought of Allen,	2	0	0
,, 24	Orphan's Tragedy,	Bought of Allen,	1	0	0
,, 25	*Jeronymo* (additions),	Ct, 10s, 10s (*see* Nov. 27, 1599),	2	0	n
Oct. 10	Rising of Cardinal Wolsey,†	Jn, 40s,	6	0	o f
		Mn, Dr, Ct, 40s; Mn, Dr, Ct, Sm, 60s; Ct, 10s; Mn, Ct, 10s,				7	19	6
,, 12	Six Clothiers,	Hg, Ht, Sm, 40s, 60s, 40s,	7	0	n
Nov. 3	Guise (Massacre of France),	Webster [Marlow revived],	...	...	...
,, 3-8	2 Six Clothiers,	Hg, Ht, Sm,	2	0	n
,, 14	Too Good to be True (Northern Man),	Ct, 5s; Ht, Sm, 50s; Ct, Ht, Sm, 70s,	6	5	f
,, 20	Vortiger,	Bought of Allen,	2	0	0
	[Crack me this] Nut,	Revived,				0	5	0
Dec. 4	Hercules,	Revived,				0	5	0
,, 14	Judas,	Br, Ry, 20s, 100s,	6	0	0	0	1	10
,, 20	Spanish Fig,	Bought of Allen,	3	0	0
Jan. 6	Prologue and Epilogue to Pontius Pilate,	Dk,,	0	10	o f
,, 12				0	0
,, 16	Tasso (altered),	Dk,,	1	0	0
,, 18	French Doctor; *Massacre of Paris*; Nut,	Bought of Allen,	6	0	0

* *See* May 27, 1600. † Both of these plays are called 'First Part.'

ADMIRAL'S PLAYERS, 23D FEBRUARY 1602 TO 12TH MARCH 1603.

First Date.	Last Date.	Name of Play.	Writers' Names and Payments.	Total Payments. £ s. d.	New or Old Play.	Money laid out. £ s. d.
Apr. 18	...	Malcolm, King of Scots,	Anon,	5 0 0	n	1 10 0
May 4	May 28	Love Parts Friendship,	Ct, Sm,	6 0 0	f	2 10 0
,, 4	July 5	Bristol Tragedy,	Dy, 20s, 40s, 40s,	5 0 0	n	
,, 5	...	Jephtha,	Mn, Dk,	5 0 0	n	13 17 0
,, 15	...	Mending 1 Cardinal Wolsey,*	Ct, .	1 0 0	o	
,, 16	June 27	Tobias,	Ct, 20s, 20s, 60s, 20s,	6 0 0	f	
,, 18	,, 2	2 Cardinal Wolsey,	. . . .	...	...	11 6 0
,, 22	...	Cesar's Fall,	Mn, Dr, Wb, Md, etc.,	5 0 0	n	
,, 29	...	Two Harpes,	Mn, Dr, Wb, Md, Dk,	3 0 0	f	
June 24	...	Richard Crookback,	} Jn, .	} 10 0 0	n	
		Additions to *Jeronymo*,			o	
July 7	...	Danish Tragedy [*Hoffmann*],	Ct, .	1 0 0	n	
,, 9	Sept. 11	Widows' Charm,	Antony [Wadeson], 10s, 5s, 10s, 5s,	1 10 0	n	
,, 19	July 31	Medicine for Curst Wife,	Dk, 40s, 40s,	4 0 0	n	
,, 29	...	Samson,	Anon,	6 0 0	f	
Aug. 8	...	Philip of Spain; Longshanks,	Bought of Allen,	4 0 0	o	
Sept. 8	...	Cartwright,	Hg,	2 10 0	n	
,, 9	Sep.15-27	Femelanco,	Rb, 60s; Ct, 10s, 50s,	6 0 0	f	6 18 0
,, 10	...	Mortimer,	Anon,	...	o	1 12 0
...	...	Earl of Hartford,	Anon,	...	n	

INTRODUCTION TO SHAKESPEARIAN STUDY. 101

Date	Title	Note	£	s	d
Sept. 27	Joshua,	Ry,	7	0	0 ƒ
Oct. 2	Tambercam,	Bought of Allen,	2	0	0 o
,, 21	Chester Tragedy (Randal, Earl of Chester),†	Md, 80s, 40s,	6	0	0 ƒ
Nov. 9	Mending Tasso,	Dk, 40s, 20s,	3	0	0 o
Dec. 4	Merry as may be (for the Court),	Dy, 40s; Dy, Sm, Ht, 120s,	8	0	0 ƒ
Nov. 17	Faustus (additions),	Bd, Rw,	4	0	0 o
,, 22	Set at Tennis,	Mn,	3	0	0 ƒ
Dec. 2	Prol. and Epil. to *Bacon* (for the Court),	Md,	0	5	0
,, 14	London Florentine,	Ct, 10s, 60s; Hy, 40s, 20s,‡	6	10	0 ƒ
,, 18	Prol. and Epil. for the Court,	Ct,	0	5	0
,, 29	*Hoffmann*,	Ct,	0	5	0 n
Jan. 29	Singer's Voluntary,	Singer,	5	0	0 n
,, 13	Like quits Like,	Ct, Hy,	2	0	0 n
,, 14	Four Sons of Aymon,	Anon,	2	0	0 o
Dec. 10 (Feb.)					
Mar. 1	Bosse of Billingsgate,	Ht, Dy, 40s, 40s; Ht, Dy, etc., 40s,	6	0	0 ƒ
,, 7	Siege of Dunkirk, with Alleyn the Pirate,	Anon,	2	0	0
,, 7	A Play Pawned with Broomfield,	Ct, §.	1	0	0 n
,, 12	2 Florentine,	Ct,	1	0	0 n

* The *Life*, or the *Rising* (?).   † Probably the *Mayor of Queenborough*.
‡ ? For the second part. The previous payment was *in full*.   § ? 2 Florentine.

MY LORD OF WORCESTER'S PLAYERS, 17TH AUGUST 1602 TO MAY 1603.

First Date.	Last Date.	Name of Play.	Writers' Names and Payments.	Total Payments. £ s. d.	New or Old Play.	Money laid out. £ s. d.
Aug. 17	Sept. 7	*Old Castle* (additions), ? 2d part,	Dk, 40s, 10s, . .	2 10 0	o	12 0 0
,, 24	...	Tragedy, ...	Ct, ...	... ...	...	3 10 0
,, 27-8	,, 27	Medicine for Curst Wife,*	Dk, 10s, 80s, 30s, and extra, 10s,	6 10 0	*f*	0 8 0
Sept. 4	...	Albert Galles, . . .	Hy, Sm, . . .	6 0 0	*f*	0 6 0
,, 7	,, 9	Robin Goodfellow,† . .	Ct, 10s, 10s, . .	1 0 0	*n*	1 6 0
,, 20	,, 30	Marshal Osric, . . .	Sm, 60s; Hy, 60s,	6 0 0	o	5 0 0
,, 20	...	Additions of Cutting Dick,	Hy, ...	1 0 0	o	3 9 0
,, 25	...	Burone [? Chapman's *Byron*],	....	... ...	*f*	
Oct. 1	Oct. 15	Two (Three) Brothers,	Sm, 40s, 40s, 40s,	6 0 0	o	0 13 0
,, 2	...	Tambercam,‡ . . .	Bought of Allen,	2 0 0	*n*	0 1 0
,, 3	...	A play, ...	Md, ...	1 0 0	...	
...	...	Berowne [? Chapman's *Byron*]	....	... ...	...	
...	...	To hang Absolom, . .				
,, 15	,, 21	Lady Jane } [*Sir Thomas Wyatt*]	Dk, Hy, Sm, Wb, 50s; Dk, Hy, Sm, Wb, Ct, 110s,	8 0 0	*f*	6 8 8
,, 27	...	2 Lady Jane }	Dk, ...	0 5 0	*n*	
Nov. 2	Nov. 26	Christmas comes but once a Year,	Hy, Wb, 60s; Dk, Ct, 40s; Ct, 40s,	7 0 0	*f*	5 0 0
,, 6	...	Overthrow of Rebels [?Lady Jane],	Ht, 40s; Ht, Dy, Sm, etc., 40s,	6 0 0	*n*	1 2 0
,, 24	Dec. 20	1 Black Dog of Newgate, .	40s, ...		*f*	
,, 24	Jan. 7	Blind eats many a Fly, .	Hy, 60s, 30s, 30s, .	6 0 0	*f*	

INTRODUCTION TO SHAKESPEARIAN STUDY. 103

Date 1	Date 2	Play	Payments	£	s	d		£	s	d
Jan. 7	Jan. 19	Unfortunate General (French History),	Ht, Sm, 30s, 30s; Ht, Sm, Dy, 40s; Ht, Sm, Dy, etc., 40s,	7	0	0	*f*	2	10	0
,, 14	...	A play,	Ct, Hy, .	2	0	0	*n*			
,, 29	Feb. 3	2 Black Dog of Newgate,	Ht, Dy, Sm, etc., 60s, 80s,	7	0	0	*f*	5	2	0
Feb. 12	Mar. 6	*Woman killed with Kindness*,	Hy, 60s, 60s,	6	0	0	*f*	7	3	0
Feb. 21	Feb. 26	2 Black Dog of Newgate (additions)	Ht, Dy, Sm, etc., 10s, 10s, 20s,	2	0	0	*f*			
Mar. 7	Mar. 12	Italian tragedy,	Sm, 40s. 80s (*see* Jan. 10, 1599),	6	0	0	*f*			
May 9	...	A play wherein Shore's Wife is written,	Ct, Dy, .	2	0	0	*n*			
	...	Baxter's Tragedy,	....	...	0	0				
1604	...	*Patient Man and Honest Whore*,	Dk, Md, .	5	0	0	*n*			

LIST OF ABBREVIATIONS OF AUTHORS' NAMES IN THE ABOVE TABLE.

Br.	Bird or Bourne, William.	Md.	Middleton, Thomas.
By.	Boyle, William.	Mn.	Munday, Antony.
Cp.	Chapman, George.	Pr.	Porter, Henry.
Ct.	Chettle, Henry.	Rb.	Robinson, Richard.
Dk.	Dekker, Thomas.	Rn.	Rankens, William.
Dr.	Drayton, Michael.	Ry.	Rowley, Samuel.
Dy.	Day, John.	Sl.	Slaughter, Martin.
Ht.	Hathaway, Richard.	Sm.	Smith, Wentworth.
Hg.	Haughton, William.	Wb.	Webster, John.
Hy.	Heywood, Thomas.	Wd.	Wadeson, Antony.
Jn.	Jonson, Benjamin.	Wl.	Wilson, Robert.

o. old, *n.* new, *f.* fully paid new play. † Probably (together with *The Devil and his Dame*) the same play as *Grim, the Collier of Croydon*. The plays with titles in italics are extant.

* See July 19, 1602.
‡ Sold also same date to Admiral's men; plot extant.

VIII.—ALLUSIONS OR SUPPOSED ALLUSIONS TO SHAKESPEARE BY CONTEMPORARIES.

'It is a common practice nowadays amongst a sort of shifting companions that run through every art and thrive by none, to leave the trade of *noverint* whereto they were born, and busy themselves with the endeavours of art, that could scarcely latinise their neck-verse if they should have need. Yet English Seneca read by candle-light yields many good sentences, as, "blood is a beggar," and so forth; and if you intreat him fair in a frosty morning he will afford you whole Hamlets, I should say handfuls, of tragical speeches.'—NASH, *Preface to Greene's Menaphon*, 1589.

'Many there be that are out of love with the obscurity wherein they live, that to win credit to their name, . . . encounter with them on whose shoulders all arts do lean. These upstart reformers of arts . . . will seem wise before their time, and now they both begin to counterfeit that which they are not, and to be ashamed of that which they are. . . . He that estimates arts by the insolence of idiots, who profess that wherein they are infants, may deem the university nought but the nurse of folly, and the knowledge of arts nought but the imitation of the stage.'—NASH, *Anatomy of Absurdity*, 1590.

'New-found songs and sonnets which every red-nose fiddler hath at his finger's end; . . . make poetry an occupation, lying is their living, and fables are their movables; . . . think knowledge a burden, tapping it before they have half tunned it, venting it before they have filled it, in whom the saying of the orator is verified: *Ante ad dicendum quam ad cognoscendam veniunt.* They come to speak before they come to know. They contemn arts as unprofitable, contenting themselves with a little country-grammar knowledge.' —NASH, *Anatomy of Absurdity*, 1590.

'Alas, poor Latinless authors. . . . For my part I do challenge no praise of learning to myself, yet have I worn a gown in the university, and so hath *caret tempus non habet moribus;* but this I dare presume, that if any Mecenas bind me to him by his bounty, or extend some sound liberality to me worth the speaking of, I will do him as much honour as any poet of my beardless years shall in England.'—NASH, *Piers Penniless*, 1592.

'Our pleasant Willy ah is dead of late,' etc.,
—SPENSER, *Tears of the Muses*, 1590,

refers probably to Lyly, who wrote no play after 1589.

'An upstart crow beautified with our feathers that, with his
"Tiger's heart wrapt in a player's hide,"
supposes he is as well able to bombast out a blank verse as the best of you, and being an absolute *Johannes Factotum*, is in his own conceit the only Shake-scene in a country.'—
GREENE, *Groatsworth of Wit*, 1592.

'About three months since died Mr Robert Greene, leaving many papers in sundry booksellers' hands, among other his *Groatsworth of Wit*, in which a letter written to divers playmakers is offensively by one or two of them taken; and because on the dead they cannot be avenged, they wilfully forge in their conceits a living author; and after tossing it to and fro, no remedy but it must needs light on me. . . . With neither of them that take offence was I acquainted, and with one of them [Marlow?] I care not if I never be. The other [Shakespeare?] whom at that time I did not so much spare as since I wish I had, . . . that I did not I am as sorry as if the original fault had been my fault; because myself have seen his demeanour no less civil than he excellent in the quality he professes. Besides, divers of worship have reported his uprightness of dealing, which argues his honesty; and his facetious grace in writing, that approves his art. . . . I protest it was all Greene's, not mine nor Master Nash's, as some unjustly have affirmed.'—
CHETTLE, *Kind-Hart's Dream*, 1592.

'Shakespeare paints poor Lucreece' rape.'
—*Willobie, his Avisa*, 1594.

'And there though last not least is Aetion,
A gentler shepherd may nowhere be found
Whose muse full of high thought's invention,
Doth like himself heroically sound.'
—SPENSER, *Colin Clout's come Home again*, 1595.

But this more likely means Drayton (Rowland) author of *Heroical Epistles* and *Idea* (ἰδέά = αἴτιον).

Kempe.—'Why, here's our fellow Shakespeare puts them all down, ay, and Ben Jonson too. Oh, that Ben Jonson is a pestilent fellow; he brought up Horace giving the poets a pill; but our fellow Shakespeare hath given him a purge that made him bewray his credit.
Burbage.— "It's a shrewd fellow, indeed."'
—*The Return from Parnassus*, 1602 (?).

'The sweet witty soul of Ovid lives in mellifluous and honey-tongued Shakespeare. Witness his *Venus and Adonis*, his *Lucreece*, his sugared *Sonnets* among his private friends, etc. . . . Shakespeare among the English is the most excellent in both kinds for the stage. For comedy, witness his *Gentlemen of Verona*, his *Errors*, his *Love Labour's Lost*, his *Love's Labour's Won*, his *Midsummer's Night Dream*, and his *Merchant of Venice;* for tragedy, his *Richard the 2, Richard the 3, Henry the 4, King John, Titus Andronicus*, and his *Romeo and Juliet*.
'The Muses would speak with Shakespeare's fine-filed phrase if they would speak English,' etc., etc.—MERES, *Palladis Tamia*, 1598.

' And Shakespeare, thou whose honey-flowing vein
   Pleasing the world thy praises doth obtain,
Whose *Venus* and whose *Lucreece* (sweet and chaste),
Thy name in Fame's immortal book have placed,' etc.
      —R. BARNEFIELD, *Poems in Divers Humors*, 1598.

'Ad Gulielmum Shakespeare.

' Honey-tongued Shakespeare, when I saw thine issue
   I swore Apollo got them and none other:
Their rosy-tainted features clothed in tissue
   Some heaven-born goddess said to be their mother:
Rose-cheekt *Adonis*, with his amber tresses,
   Fair fire-hot *Venus*, charming him to love her
Chaste *Lucretia*, virgin-like her dresses,
   Proud, lust-stung *Tarquin* seeking still to prove her;
Romeo, Richard, more whose names I know not,
   Their sugared tongues and power-attractive beauty,
Say they are saints, although that saints they show not,
   For thousands vows to them subjective duty;
They burn in love thy children, Shakespeare, het them,
Go woo thy Muse! More nymphish brood beget them!
      —WEEVER, *Epigrams*, 1596.

' Players, I love ye and your quality,
   As ye are men that pastime not abused,
 And some I love for painting, poesy,   (W. S. R. B.*)
   And say fell Fortune cannot be excused,
   That hath for better uses you refused.
 Wit, courage, good shape, good parts, and all good
   As long as all these goods are no worse used,
 And though the stage doth stain pure gentle blood,
   Yet generous ye are in mind and mood.'
            —JOHN DAVIES of Hereford, *Microcosmos*, 1603.

' Nor doth the silver-tonguèd *Melicert*
   Drop from his honey'd Muse one sable tear
 To mourn her death that gracèd his desert
   And to his lays opened her royal ear.
 Shepherd, remember our *Elizabeth*,
 And sing her rape done by that *Tarquin*, Death!'
            —HENRY CHETTLE, *England's Mourning
                            Garment*, 1603.

'There shalt thou learn to be frugal (for players were never so thrifty as they are now about London), and to feed upon all men, to let none feed upon thee, to make thy hand a stranger to thy pocket, thy heart slow to perform thy tongue's promise; and when thou feelest thy purse well lined, buy thee some place of lordship in the country, that, growing weary of playing, thy money may then bring thee to dignity and reputation; then thou needest care for no man; no, not for them that before made thee proud with speaking their words on the stage. Sir, I thank you (quoth the player) for this good counsel. I promise you I will make use of it, for I have heard, indeed, of some that have gone to London very meanly, and have come in time to be exceeding wealthy.'
—*Ratsei's Ghost*, 1605-6.

' You poets all, brave Shakespeare,
       Jonson, Greene,
   Bestow your time to write
       For England's Queen.'
            —*A Mournful Ditty*, etc., 1603.

---

* That is, William Shakespeare, Richard Burbadge, who is said to have painted Shakespeare's portrait.

' *To our English Terence, Mr Will Shakespeare.*
' Some say, good Will, which I in sport do sing,
    Hadst thou not played some kingly parts in sport
Thou hadst been a companion for a king,
    And been a king among the meaner sort.
Some others rail; but rail as they think fit,
Thou hast no railing but a reigning wit;
And honesty thou sow'st which they do reap,
So to increase their stock which they do keep.'
        —JOHN DAVIES, *Scourge of Folly*, 1607.

' Some followed her [Fortune] by acting all men's parts;
    These on a stage she raised (in scorn) to fall,
And made them mirrors by their acting arts
    Wherein men saw their faults, though ne'er so small.
Yet some she guerdon'd not to their deserts, (W. S. R. B.*)
    But other some were but ill action all,
Who, while they acted ill, ill stayed behind,
By custom of their manner in their mind.'
        —J. DAVIES, *Humours Heaven on Earth*, 1609.

' That full and heightened style of Master Chapman, the laboured and understanding works of Master Jonson, the no less worthy composures of the both worthily excellent Master Beaumont and Master Fletcher; and lastly (without wrong last to be named), the right happy and copious industry of Master Shakespeare, Master Dekker, and Master Heywood.'
—JOHN WEBSTER, *Dedication to the White Devil*, 1612.

' *To Master Wm. Shakespeare.*

' Shakespeare, that nimble Mercury, thy brain,
    Lulls many hundred Argus' eyes asleep:
So fit for all thou fashionest thy vein,
    At th' horse-foot fountain thou hast drunk full deep.
Virtue's or vice's theme to thee all one is:
    Who loves chaste life, there's *Lucreece* for a teacher;
Who lists read lust, there's *Venus and Adonis*,
    True model of a most lascivious lecher;
Besides, in plays thy wit winds like Meander,
    Whence needy new composers borrow more

---

* William Shakespeare, Richard Burbadge.

Than Terence doth from Plautus or Menander,
  But to praise thee aright I want thy store.
Then let thine own work thine own worth upraise,
  And help t' adore thee with deservèd days.'
—THYRSIS. FREEMAN, *Rub and a Great Cast*, 1614.

' To him that impt my fame with Clio's quill,
  Whose magic raised me from Oblivion's den,
That writ my story on the Muses' hill,
  And with my actions dignified his pen;
He that from Helicon sends many a rill,
  Whose nectar'd veins are drunk by thirsty men,
Crown'd be his style with fame, his head with bays,
And none detract but gratulate his praise.

' Yet if his scenes have not engrost all grace,
  The much famed actor could expend on stage,
If Time or Memory have left a place
  For me to fill t' inform this ignorant age;
In that intent I show my horrid face,
  Imprest with fear and characters of rage,
Nor acts nor chronicles could e'er contain
The hell-deep reaches of my soundless brain.'
—C. B., *The Ghost of Richard III*, 1614.

                    ' A hall, a hall!
Room for the spheres, the orbs celestial
Will dance Kemp's jig. They'll revel with neat jumps;
A worthy poet hath put on their pumps.
O wit's quick travers, but *sance ceo's* slow,
Good faith, 'tis hard for nimble Curio.
Ye gracious orbs, keep the old measuring,
All's spoiled if once ye fall to capering.
    Luscus, what's played to-day? Faith, now I know;
I set thy lips abroach, from whence doth flow
Nought but pure *Juliet and Romeo*.
Say who acts best, Drusus or Roscio?

' Now I have him that ne'er of aught did speak
  But when of plays or players he did treat.
H'ath made a commonplace book out of plays,
  And speaks in print, at least whate'er he says
Is warranted by Curtain *plaudities*.
If ere you heard him courting Lesbia's eyes,

Say, courteous sir, speaks he not movingly
From out some new pathetic tragedy?
He writes, he rails, he jests, he courts, what not,
And all from out his huge long-scrapèd stock
Of well-penn'd plays.'
—MARSTON, *Scourge of Villainy.*
Satire x, 1598.

' A man, a man, a kingdom for a man.'
—*From the same*, Satire vii.

SUPPLEMENTARY CHAPTER.

SHAKESPEARE'S PLOTS: HOW ARE THEY CONNECTED?

THE publication, by Mr Furness, of the *Variorum* edition of some of the master-pieces of Shakespeare, has brought prominently into relief the fact that commentaries on our world-poet, especially of the æsthetic kind, already far exceed the limits which the shortness of life and the pressure of everyday business impose on ordinary readers. The enormous number of volumes (over 6000) already collected in the Shakespeare Memorial Library, at Birmingham, which is still acknowledged to be far from complete, yet further impresses on us the partial and fragmentary results as yet attained by these voluminous investigations, and the undying interest that attaches to the subject. Yet among all the scholia, essays, and treatises, so largely accumulated; varying as they do from mere statement of subjective impression to elaborate statistical tables of more or less valuable metrical or linguistic peculiarities; there is not one that satisfactorily traces, there are only few that even attempt to trace, what on the face of the matter would seem to be one of the most simple, and also of the most interesting lines of investigation that the subject admits of—the connection, logical and chronological, of the *plots* of the plays. Many suggestive comparisons of special incidents and characters, many little links between various comedies and tragedies, have been indeed afforded us; but no broad, general treatment has been adapted, which would give us a bird's-eye view of the general progress and development of our dramatist in this particular. The present chapter is an attempt to supply this deficiency.

Before entering on the main subject it will be well to say a few words on the classification of the plays here adopted. We are so familiar with the division made by the folio editors into comedies, histories, and tragedies, that it seems an act of supererogation, if not of arrogance, to propose a new one.

Yet the objections to that arrangement are weighty and numerous. A classification which separates *Cymbeline* as a tragedy from *Winter's Tale* as a comedy, and leaves *Pericles* either unclassed as a 'play,' or inserts it, as most editors do, in the tragedies, is eminently unsatisfactory. If any three of our author's works are specially bound together by similarities of situation and treatment, it is the three here mentioned. Again, *Richard II* and *Richard III*, which are tragedies pure and simple, and are so called in the original quarto editions, are not placed in the tragedy group; while *Julius Cæsar*, allied as it is, in metre, handling, and conception to *Henry V*, is separated from it on the superficial ground that the one treating of English history, and the other of Roman, they must be looked on, not as belonging to sub-classes of one division, but as belonging to divisions so separate as to include *Lear* and *Macbeth* in the one, and the *Henry IV-V* trilogy in the other. Or if the ground ridiculed by Shakespeare himself—

> 'Tragical, my lord, it is,
> For Pyramus therein doth kill himself,'

be relied on; if *Julius Cæsar* is to be a tragedy on the ground of his assassination and Brutus's suicide; if *Cymbeline* is a tragedy because the Queen and Cloten do not live to the end of the play,—then why is not *Pericles* a tragedy because Leonine is killed, or *Winter's Tale* because Antigonus is eaten by a bear? It is clear that if this method be adopted for our classification, we must introduce a new class of tragi-comedy, as Fletcher and others did. And then, where shall we stop? shall we go into pastoral, and pastoral-comical, and all the other sub-divisions satirised in *Hamlet?* Shall we separate until our classes are nearly as numerous as our plays? Finally it is not possible to treat satisfactorily such a play as *Romeo and Juliet*, apart from the *Two Gentlemen of Verona* and the *Merchant of Venice*, between which it demonstratively stands chronologically, and with both of which it is manifestly connected in manner of treatment and in characterisation: it is not possible to separate *Othello* from the other plays treating of the same subject—jealousy; merely on the ground that these two plays end in sorrow and death, and the others in life and joy. We must classify, not by the accidental, but the essential; the nature of the chief passions brought into play, and the manner of their treatment in the dramas themselves. Schlegel saw this long since as regards these two latter plays, and has some very sensible observations on the subject.

I propose, then, to adopt two classes, and two only. The former dealing with romance and fable, founded on poems and novels, treating of love and jealousy as one, if not the chief, of our businesses in life; the latter dealing with fact and history, founded on biography and chronicle, treating of public affairs and the life of the nation as affected by the actions of the chief men therein prominent. This latter class comprises all the histories, commonly so called, the three Roman plays, *Timon*, and the great tragedies, *Hamlet*, *Lear*, and *Macbeth*. It is worth while, however, to notice that all recent chronological investigation founded on external evidence, points to the conclusion that one play of each of these classes was produced, or at least revived, annually, thus agreeing with the old tradition that Shakespeare for the most part wrote two plays per year for the stage, during the time that he was connected with it.

I now come to the consideration of the plots of the plays taken individually. There can be little doubt that the earliest was *Love's Labour's Lost;* but since this play was re-written in 1597, as we are told on the title-page of the quarto, it will be most convenient to treat of it at that date. It will suffice to note here, that in its want of individual character in the chief personages, in its superficiality of feeling, in its intricacy of cross-purposed plot, it belongs to the same group as the two plays that immediately succeed it.

Midsummer Night's Dream is connected in its general formation with the foregoing, by the following particulars. It has the same general pervading sense of cross-purposed wooing as a foundation; the same limitation of the action within a narrow period of time; the same introduction of a performance by the burlesque portion of the characters to enhance the comicality of the concluding scenes; the same ridicule of the humours of the life of the lower portions of the community in contrast to the higher aristocracy; the same setting of the whole action in a framework expounded in the initial and concluding scenes. Yet there is little advance in dramatic power, however it may excel in poetic worth, as separated from dramatic. The most effective acting scenes, as well as the most characteristic, are the two rehearsals by Bottom and his fellows, and it is impossible to say how far these have been modified in later revisions before the play was published in 1600. They certainly show a deeper knowledge of human nature than anything else in the earliest plays of Shakespeare.

The *Comedy of Errors*, which forms a distinct link between the preceding and following plays, has more dramatic excellence. Comparatively weak as a poem, it yet gives us the earliest intimation of the suitability of Shakespeare's genius to the stage. The characters do more and declaim less than in the two earlier plays; yet the cross purposes, the time-limit, the framework, are so like the *Midsummer Night's Dream* as to distinctly point to an almost contemporaneous origin. The introductory scenes especially are nearly identical in motive. Nor is it unworthy of notice that in this play Pinch, the schoolmaster, is ridiculed for a bearded doctor:

> 'A hungry, lean-faced villain,
> A mere anatomy, a mountebank,
> A threadbare juggler, and a fortune-teller,
> A needy, hollow-eyed sharp-looking wretch,
> A living dead-man'

—just as Holofernes, the schoolmaster in *Love's Labour's Lost*, is shown up for his pedantry. Having 'been at a great feast of languages, and stolen the scraps,' he gives us words and phrases from French, Latin, Italian, and Spanish, to an extent unparalleled in the other plays, even by Pistol. After this date (1593-4) there is no ridicule of schoolmasters in Shakespeare.

The main plot of *Twelfth Night* is so closely connected with the *Comedy of Errors*, on the one hand—by the incident of the shipwreck which separates the twins, and still more so by the introduction of the twins themselves and the consequent errors that arise therefrom; and, on the other hand, with the *Two Gentlemen of Verona*—by the wooing of a lady by a girl in boy's disguise in behalf of the man with whom the girl is herself in love—that it is difficult not to believe that some portion of the play was written at this date. As the whole play was, however, produced unquestionably some seven years later, and if any part of it is of the earlier date, it was revised and re-written at the later, I leave the consideration of it as more suited for the later place in which it certainly must come in a list of the plays, arranged in date of production.

But as to the place of the *Two Gentlemen of Verona* there can be no doubt. It is the earliest completed specimen of the series of comedies in which we meet with the disguised maiden that attends her lover as a page, who is so prominent in stage plots through all the subsequent history of the drama. This play is rather a friendship than a love play. The falsehood of Proteus is its central motive. It is the first of Shakespeare's productions which have really a right to the title of a comedy. The preceding plays have no complete story founded on human life; they are merely dramatised incidents, or exceptional events, which in inferior hands would have given rise at most to an interlude or farce. Here, however, we have a true comedy of life, founded on a novel. Yet the thread of continuity of development is not broken. The Dromios are reproduced in Launce and Speed; Luce reappears as Lucetta. In all these we can trace the beginnings of the clowns and waiting-maids who so often are introduced in subsequent comedies. Nor has the cross-wooing which Ben Jonson reprobated yet died out, though it never reappears after this play in similar fashion. The introduction of burlesque characters, pedants, and country actors, who have no natural connection with the plot, now gives way to the comedy of servants or clowns who are necessarily attached to the principal personages. This system also had to run its course and become obsolete, but it is a distinct step in advance; as indeed is the whole of the play, looked on from a stage point of view.

In *Romeo and Juliet* we find much of the work in the *Two Gentlemen of Verona* taken up and improved. Not only in special incidents, such as the visiting of the lover to the lady by means of a rope ladder, the banishments of Valentine and Romeo, the introduction of friars on the stage, but in the very marrow of the plots, we find that this play is a development of the preceding. As Proteus forsakes Julia, Romeo gives up Rosaline; as Valentine inveighs against love to Proteus, so does Mercutio to Romeo. In fact, in all the early part of the play the parallelism between these two pairs of characters is accurately maintained. In the later portions the tragical turn given to the *dénouement* of course interferes with this, but no one can read the two plays consecutively without being struck by the similarities here mentioned.

In the *Merchant of Venice* we find still further development. This play, like the *Two Gentlemen of Verona*, is a friendship play, though in this case the friend is faithful, in the other faithless; just as in *Romeo and Juliet* the lady is faithful to her lover, while in *Troylus and Cressida* she is not so. This was pointed out by me in an article in the *Academy;* but I was mistaken in supposing that plays of mutual contrast were generally produced successively. This was seldom the case, and development of other kinds must be first looked for. There can, however, be little doubt that the *Merchant of Venice* was subsequent to the *Two Gentlemen of Verona.* The characters, though cast in the same mould, are more highly finished. Nerissa is as superior to Lucetta as Portia is to Julia. We have here again a disguised woman, but disguised for a worthier motive. Launcelot is an improvement on the hitherto unnecessarily doubled men-servants, and a nearer approach to the clown of subsequent plays. If a direct comparison be sought between portions of plays, no better example could be chosen than the discussions between the ladies and their waiting-maids on the characters of the suitors in I, ii, and in *Two Gentlemen of Verona,* I, ii.

Much Ado about Nothing has been shown by Mr Brae to be the same play as *Love's Labour's Won.* The allusions to this former title in II, i, 380, V, i, 291, are conclusive on this point, even if there were no such parallelism of character as that between Berowne and Rosaline with Benedick and Beatrice. But the reproduction of *Love's Labour's Lost* in 1597, and the mention by Meres of *Love's Labour's Won* in 1598, fix the date of this latter play, if identical with *Much Ado about Nothing,* to be in the latter year. It would be useless to go over the ground so carefully traversed by Mr Brae as to the contrast between these two plays. It will be better to show how in other parts of the plot, or rather in the second plot, it serves as an introduction to the play that succeeds it, the *Merry Wives of Windsor.* In both we have the same principal motive, jealousy, founded on the information of a rascal; in both, the same ridicule of inefficient administrators of public justice; though, indeed, as far as the foolish constable is concerned, this rather gives us an additional link with *Love's Labour's Lost,* as revised in 1597. But above all, in these two plays there is distinct reference to the stage war going on between Jonson and Marston, Dekker, & Co.; for that 'Deformed who has been a vile thief these seven year' alludes to the name given by the Chapel Children's playwrights to Shakespeare himself, is as probable, or rather certain, as that Nym, with eternal repetition of 'that's the humour of it,' would be in 1599 (the certain date of *Henry V,* and almost certain of the *Merry Wives of Windsor*) regarded as an allusion to Jonson's two humour plays, one dating

1598, the other 1599. If, however, we look earlier for the play that is to be regarded as the precursor of *Much Ado about Nothing*, we shall find it, not in the *Merchant of Venice*, but in *Romeo and Juliet*. The friars, the dirges at the tombs, the descriptions of mourning, are extremely similar in both plays, and should be carefully compared. This applies, however, only to the main plot. The other, as has been pointed out, is a parallel to *Love's Labour's Lost*.

The *Merry Wives of Windsor* is so intimately connected in many of its characters with the historical trilogy of *Henry IV-V* that it would in some respects be better considered along with them. We must here, however, notice not only its general likeness to *Much Ado about Nothing*, which indeed would have served as a title for this play, but its special likeness to preceding plays in some of its minor characters. It contains a braggart and a curate, just as *Love's Labour's Lost*, which had been so lately revised by Shakespeare. Mrs Quickly is far more like the nurse in *Romeo and Juliet* than she is to any preceding character in the comedies—indeed in some respects more like than she is to herself as represented in the histories; and Robin the page is a reproduction of the boy who waits on Armado. We find also in Pistol and Evans the tendency to give snatches of foreign languages that is so abundantly displayed in *Love's Labour's Lost*, and which is never shown afterwards, except in a much slighter degree in *Twelfth Night*.

Of the *Taming of the Shrew*, which is, as far as Shakespeare is concerned, merely a re-writing of an older piece, which preceded all the comedies we generally recognise as of his production, it will be sufficient to note that although it clearly cannot be recognised as belonging to the regular series of his work, it yet so far agrees with its chronological position that it is, like the *Merry Wives of Windsor*, a comedy of middle-class life, unromantic, not dealing with dukes and kings, and that it has in it, as principal among the subordinate personages, a servant, Grumio, who is remodelled from the Saunder of the old play into something like the Gratiano of the *Merchant of Venice;* changed from the type which Lyly and Lodge had given us into that of the true Shakespearian coinage.

But in *As You Like It* the thread of development is again easy to untwist; the position between the *Merchant of Venice* and *Twelfth Night* is definitely assignable. This

and the succeeding plays are essentially the two love-plays
of Shakespeare, above all others, far more so even than
Romeo and Juliet. For in other plays it is the passion of the
senses, or the jealousy of possession, or the enthralment of
the fancy, that is displayed. In these it is the congruence and
complemental perfection of the two halves of perfect being
that have found their match. In *As You Like It* the aspect
of love dwelt on is the love at first sight celebrated by Marlow, the dead shepherd of III, v, 83; in *Twelfth Night* it is
the patient waiting and the entire devotion of the lover. In
both it is the woman who woos; in both she is disguised in
man's attire; in both the most perfect descriptions of the
passion in its purity are given that poet has ever penned. In
the subordinate parts of these plays there is also great similarity. The two most perfect clowns in all Shakespeare's works
are to be found in them, Touchstone and Feste; in both we
find—instead of the ridicule of pedantry or ignorance of the
earlier plays, or the allusions to outside quarrels of those
immediately preceding—that self-conceit and folly are held
up to scorn, by precept in Jaques, by example in Malvolio.
The curate, the country wench, and the bumpkin, Sir Oliver,
William, and Audrey, should be compared with Sir Nathaniel,
Costard, and Jaquenetta in *Love's Labour's Lost*, more for
their difference than their likeness. That earliest play seems
to have been used by Shakespeare in one way or other as
suggestive of subsequent characters or situations more than
all the rest.

The similarity of part of *Twelfth Night* to *Two Gentlemen
of Verona* has already been noticed. Compare also Viola's
description of herself (II, iv, 110-121) with Julia's in the *Two
Gentlemen* (IV, iv, 150-177). The duel between Viola and
Sir Andrew is evidently a development of the humour of
mine host in the affray between the doctor and the parson
in the *Merry Wives of Windsor*.

In *All's Well that Ends Well* the clown, although somewhat inferior, is no unworthy successor to Touchstone and
Feste, and clearly belongs to the same series. Parolles is a
development of Armado rather than of Pistol, with whom he
has been often compared; but the trick played on him, and
his exposure, is of the same mint, and I should say nearly
contemporary, with the device of Maria and Sir Toby against
Malvolio. Maria, by the way, is the last of the series of
pert waiting-women. The meeting of Helen with her hostess
is extremely like that between Julia and the host in the *Two
Gentlemen of Verona*. The clear existence of two styles in

this play, one quite early, has led to the opinion that it is a recast of *Love's Labour's Won;* but as there is no reason whatever to suppose that that play was ever recast, and there are allusions to the present title of *All's Well that Ends Well* in the parts of the play that are in the early manner, there is no reason for differing from the opinion of Mr Brae, as quoted above.

That *Measure for Measure* followed closely on *All's Well that Ends Well* can hardly be doubted by any one who compares carefully the handling of the final scenes, which are almost identical in treatment. The device of the substitution of the real wife for the supposed maiden victim is also alike in both plays. The foolish constable Elbow, and the introduction of friars, carry us back to *Much Ado about Nothing* for a parallel. The inferiority of the constable has always been a stumbling-block with critics who hold that Shakespeare must have improved in *all* respects throughout the whole of his career. But even granting this doubtful proposition, there is no difficulty in the matter. It is clear that characters ought not to be compared in respect of excellence of development, unless they are not only similar in nature, but are also introduced under similar circumstances, and are of like importance in the plot. We might as well complain that the clown in *Othello* is not the equal of Touchstone. In this play we miss our clown proper, who is poorly replaced by Pompey, an inferior kind of a male Mrs Quickly. In fact, the interest of Shakespeare is more and more absorbed at this stage of his development by the main plot, to the exclusion of any lower secondary scenes.

In *Othello* this is still more manifest. The clown sinks into the smallest proportions. The subject of jealousy was probably suggested by the fact that in the previous year Shakespeare had had to re-write the *Merry Wives of Windsor*, and he felt that he had not treated the passion of jealousy seriously enough in that play. *Othello*, like *Romeo and Juliet*, is a romantic, not an historical or semi-historical play, and serves as a demarcation between the comedies proper and all that succeed in the series as I arrange it. For, explain the fact how we will, no comedy, strictly so called, occurs after *Measure for Measure*. Whether the fashion of the time demanded a mixture of tragedy, or Shakespeare's own inclination led him at the age of forty to take a more serious view of life, from this date we have only tragical histories and tragi-comedies from his hand. In this play we have his last clown. For comparison with earlier plays, besides the main subject of jealousy, the relation of Roderigo to Iago should be studied alongside with that of Sir Andrew Aguecheek to Sir Toby Belch. The slight clown-scene has its counterpart also in *Twelfth Night*, and a still earlier one in *Romeo and Juliet*. Iago should of course be compared also with Don John in *Much Ado about Nothing*.

The remaining plays are closely connected. *Pericles*, the earliest of them, is connected with *Measure for Measure*, by the leaving a deputy behind to govern during the prince's absence; but this, as well as the similarity of the names Escanes and Escalus, Marina and Mariana, is only a superficial resemblance. We evidently, in these last plays, pass into a different world. Events are in them ruled by the interference of the deities. Man's will is nothing; fate is all. Man may strive, but oracles must be fulfilled. Oracles, prophecies, augurs, magic, are the means of ascertaining the will of the gods. The gods are pagan. Juno, Jupiter, Ceres, Diana, are now actors on the scene, not fables to be alluded to. Magic is a real power over elemental spirits, not a mere delusion of the devil. There are more beings on earth than man—misshapen Caliban, sylphed Ariel; not merely mischievous fairies and fiend-worshipping witches, but spirits that can be brought under man's power by lawful magic; and gods that care for, and interfere with man's destiny. It is the world of the Rosicrucians and the Greek mythology rolled into one, not that of the Teutonic traditions, and the semi-scriptural witches. In *Pericles* it is Diana; in *Cymbeline*, Jupiter; in *Winter's Tale*, Apollo; in the *Tempest*, the magician, who rule and prophesy. The priest, the augur, the sybil, are their instruments; their means of communication are dreams, visions, and oracles; and above all, man himself

> 'is of such stuff
> As dreams are made of, and our little life
> Is rounded with a sleep.'

The plots too are all of the same texture; reunions of parents and children are given, as in Marina, Guiderius, Arviragus, and Perdita; reunions of wives and husbands in Thaisa and Hermione; recovery of lost dignities in the sons of Cymbeline, and the daughters of Leontes, Pericles, and Prospero; recoveries from supposed death in Marina, Imogen, and Perdita, in Thaisa and Hermione. The play of *Cymbeline* is like that of *Pericles* in the visions given to Posthumus and

Pericles while asleep ; and in all this play the conduct of the story holds an intermediate place between *Pericles* and *Winter's Tale*. The wicked queen corresponds to Dionyza, and attempts to kill Imogen, as the other does Perdita. The physician in these plays should also be compared.

In *Winter's Tale* we have the same main motive as in *Cymbeline*—jealousy; but the singular division of the play into two as it were, by passing over some sixteen years, brings it close to *Pericles*. So does the seclusion of the queens supposed dead. The reunions at the close are most alike in these two plays.

In the *Tempest* we have a sea-scene as we have in *Pericles*. In fact the last-named play, like *Love's Labour's Lost*, seems to have been used up by Shakespeare as a series of suggestions for characters in subsequently written plays. Even the pretended anger of Prospero with Ferdinand for loving his daughter, is a reproduction of the situation between Simonides and Pericles, in a scene certainly not written by Shakespeare even to the extent of a single line.

Thus far, then, I have endeavoured to show by a number of minor considerations, how each romantic play is to some extent a development of various parts of those that preceded it. Let us now, for a moment, examine more broadly the chronological arrangement thus attained. If the arrangement be a true one, it gives in succession the following groups. Firstly, three plays which are eminent for their want of dramatic experience, and the embroiled, or rather intertangled nature of their plots ; then a group of four plays which have for subjects, one pair faithlessness, the other pair fidelity, in love and friendship. These are succeeded by two plays on jealousy and two on love in its most perfect forms. We next come to two in which faithful wives succeed in regaining their faithless husbands.

Then another pair (one of them an earlier play revived) treating of jealousy in its comic and tragic aspects ; finally a group of four plays which dwell on reunion after separation, and look forward to rest as the highest reward. There is even in this slight outline a method, a progress visible. Only on reading the whole series consecutively can we feel how the many subtle links that connect a man's works when read in chronological order start out into clearness, and are at once recognised. These cannot be shown in one chapter : but on the other hand, the order here proposed can be tested by different considerations.

We may, for instance, test it by external data of chronology.

The dates of about one-third of these plays are known within a year, and the fact that six (or seven counting *Love's Labour's Won*) are mentioned by Meres in 1598, fixes these as first in the list. Compare then the following enumeration in which the dates of the plays in italics are definitely certain, the others conjectural, and the plays given by Meres separated by a line thus : |.

'Love's Labour's Lost,' 1592 ; 'Midsummer Night's Dream,' 1593; *Comedy of Errors, 1593-4;* 'Two Gentlemen of Verona,' 1595 ; *Romeo and Juliet, 1596;* 'Merchant of Venice,' 1597 ; 'Much Ado about Nothing,' 1598 ; | *Merry Wives of Windsor*, first version, *1599;* 'As You Like It,' 1600 ; *Taming of the Shrew, 1600-1;* 'Twelfth Night,' 1601 ; 'All's Well that Ends Well,' 1602 ; *Measure for Measure, 1603;* Merry Wives of Windsor, second version, *1604;* 'Othello,' 1605-6 ; 'Troylus and Cressida,' 1605-6 ; *Pericles, 1606;* 'Cymbeline,' 1608-9 ; *Winter's Tale, 1610-11; Tempest, 1611.*

It is clear that this series corresponds with that derived from the examination we have given of the plots. Or again we may test it by its agreement or non-agreement with the known development of Shakespeare's metrical system; not the so-called development which would assign different dates to two plays, because one has some half-dozen rhymes or weak endings more than the other; but the clearly-marked division into groups and periods in each of which distinct manners of versification were adopted by the poets. It will be found that these periods coincide with the order of the above list, and end respectively with the years 1596, 1601, 1606, each period of five years containing about five plays ; or if for convenience of memory we relegate the *Taming of the Shrew* to the date of its earliest form, and insert in the last period the *History of Cardenio*, by Fletcher and Shakespeare, now lost, each period will contain exactly five plays. This looks artificial, but for that very reason it is useful as a mnemonical device.

Or again, we may examine the list to see if certain kinds of characters, such as clowns for instance, that were fashionable at certain epochs, are brought together chronologically in the table : we shall find they are ; and many other modes of examination will no doubt suggest themselves to the reader of Shakespeare, which will put the arrangement now suggested to a conclusive ordeal.

But as my object is not to advocate any special chronological arrangement, and so bring myself within the danger of the specialists in such studies, but rather to give the ordinary reader such hints as I have myself found useful in studying these plays in a certain order, I will here leave this part of the subject for more limited and less critical considerations.

It will or may of course be urged against such speculations as are contained in this chapter, that they are void of practical utility; that any work of art should be judged *per se;* if it be beautiful, we enjoy it; if not, we avoid it. What matter how and when it was produced? Our delight in a thing of beauty is independent of all critical or historical associations. This might be answered in many ways. It will suffice here to suggest that this view may be true for smaller or sketchier productions. We do not care for the biography of a man who invents a pattern for a wine-glass, or writes a magazine article, or sketches a bit of roadside bank, however well these things be done. Nor do we feel much interest in the compiler of a fashionable novel, or the anonymous critic of a weekly journal. But in the authors of the masterpieces of human effort, the Phidiases, the Raffaelles, the Beethovens, the Shakespeares, men do feel an imperishable interest; every new factor, new combination of facts, concerning these men is lit up and ennobled by the halo that encircles the men themselves; hence it comes that every new point of view to which we can attain, from which their works are visible, produces in us a feeling akin to that which we have in looking at a landscape already familiar in all its details, but now seen from some hill-top or place of vantage, to which we have climbed for the first time. And so it ought to be. It is better to know a few things well, than many things imperfectly,—better in the sense of giving us more delight independently of the training we gain in the process of learning; and in these days when epics and tragedies have attained to such a feverish development, that a single poem equal in magnitude to some six of Shakespeare's masterpieces, can be turned out of the manufactory in a year or two by men far younger than Shakespeare was when he wrote his first-fruits of his invention, it may be well to turn to our *Canterbury Tales, Fairy Queen,* and *Lear,* to ascertain how the men worked, whose work has lived while the *Leonidases* and *Festuses* and *Joan of Arcs* have vanished from the memory of men, and from the shelves of the library.

Let us now turn to the historical series, which will require a shorter treatment for our present purpose, both because the order is less doubtful and the plots of histories are necessarily less intimately connected in manner of treatment.

In the Talbot episode of 1 *Henry VI*, the earliest work which we can confidently assign to Shakespeare, we find him so imbued with the manner of his predecessors, that, excepting in trenchant energy, there is little to distinguish his work as yet from that of Peele. He seems, like Turner, to have deliberately written in rivalry to each of his precursors before adopting a decisive manner of his own. This is still more strongly shown in *Richard II*, which is as certainly a rival piece to Marlow's *Edward II* as the *Merchant of Venice* is to the *Jew of Malta*, or *Love's Labour's Lost* to the plays of Lyly. In fact, the likeness is so strong as at times to give one the impression that some of Marlow's work is contained in the Shakespearian plays (see Marlow's *Edward II*, in Collins' series). Again in *Edward III* the episode of the Countess of Salisbury is, I think, meant to rival the scenes between the King and Ida in Greene's *James IV of Scotland*. *Richard III* (whether founded on a sketch of Peele's or not) is a completion of as well as a competitor with 2 and 3 *Henry VI*, by Peele and Marlow; *King John* is a still more strongly marked challenge to the author of the *Troublesome Reign of King John* (perhaps G. Peele); and the *Henry IV-V* trilogy so eclipses the *Famous Victories of Henry V* that it is scarcely possible to read the older play with patience. Yet although all these histories were written successively in rivalry with others, there is a distinct development visible in Shakespeare's work. The unmixed tragedy of the fates of Talbot and the Richards, is replaced by the mixed comedy and tragedy of John and the Henries. Rightly are the latter called lives, not tragedies. Faulconbridge and Falstaff teach us the many-sidedness of life, and the inadequacy of any art which develops one side only in each of its productions to give us that large view of man and the world which has been attained by Shakespeare, and in a less degree by Göthe. Taken simply as a comic dramatist, Molière is greater than Shakespeare; merely as a tragic dramatist, Sophocles is his superior; but as an expounder of life in its totality, the only names that I can place near him are those of Göthe, Balzac, Fielding, and R. Browning.

Immediately after these histories proper, we come on a group of plays which we may call the ghost series. *Cæsar*, *Richard III*, second version, *Macbeth*, *Hamlet*. It is scarcely necessary to point out how the conception of a ghost acquires greater objectivity through this series. A mere subjective vision in *Cæsar* acquiring more definite form in *Richard III*, from being seen by Richmond as well as Richard, gains additional horror from the supernatural surroundings in *Macbeth*.* In *Hamlet* the vision has an objective existence, and is seen by all present, except in the closet-scene where the guilty queen is blind to it. It is more important to note that the three first of this group are all ambition plays. Cæsar's is a covetous ambition, he wants the world to be his that he may do what he likes with it, quite irrespective of others, and the reaction of democratic feeling, excited by him, destroys him. He is slain by patriots. Richard's ambition is revengeful. The world hates him for his deformity; he wants power to avenge himself on the world; this makes him cruel; his cruelty makes men hate him, and he is slain by a rival. Macbeth's ambition is an envious one, he does not see why another man should be better used by fate than himself; his envy leads him to murder and usurpation, and hence his destruction. He is, like Richard, slain by the rightful heir. That these plays were produced in succession† there can be no doubt; and it would not be difficult (had we space) to show the connection between the subjects of these plays and the political events of the years in which they were produced.

From disappointed ambition we pass in the play of *Hamlet* to disappointed love. *Hamlet* is connected with *Macbeth* in its outer plot by its ghost, as with *Lear* by the madness depicted in it; but more deeply with the latter in the deep philosophy and consummate insight into the human heart. These two plays are Shakespeare's masterpieces. The philosophic sloth of Hamlet, and the unbridled wrath of Lear, lead alike to their ruin. In both cases the unreliability of ties of blood is the primary cause of their destruction. Still Lear has a daughter that loves him, and Hamlet a friend. Timon has neither. Lear trusts his daughters that flatter him, and Timon his parasites, and both are forsaken when they have no more to give.

The two next plays form a minor group, taken from Roman history. They contain histories of two great men, evidently favourites of Shakespeare's, who fail in their aspirations through positive vices of their own—Antony from lust, Coriolanus from pride. The similarities of handling in these

* Banquo's ghost is seen by Macbeth only, but the Weyard Sisters by Banquo as well.

† *Richard III*, of course, being a revival.

plays have often been pointed out. All through this series of tragedies (including the Roman histories) the pervading idea is that the dram of alloy makes brittle all the noble metal. The chief character in each of these plays is endowed with noble qualities, but he has one defect. This brings him into collision with the unyielding law of the universe, and the weaker goes to the wall.*

The only two plays left to mention have been altered by Fletcher. But it is clear from the parts left of Shakespeare's writing, that in them we have not his best work. His hand shows comparative failure in *Henry VIII*,—failure in characterisation, plot, and absence of humour; but in the *Two Noble Kinsmen* there is worse failure than that of execution, there is failure in conception. In spite of many admirable touches in the first act, there is a coarseness, or rather a want of sensibility, in many places; and the poet who conceived and partly wrote the part of the Jailer's daughter, after having written Ophelia, did well to retire from his vocation before his power had altogether decayed.

In this chapter I have endeavoured to point out the two classes into which Shakespeare's plays are divisible, and the order in which they should be æsthetically studied, which I believe coincides nearly with the chronological order. But let no one suppose that I mean to give an æsthetic commentary on them; that has been done with more or less success by others, with whom I certainly shall not endeavour to compete. Nor do I think it desirable that the student should trouble himself about such criticisms till he has formed an independent judgment of his own. Above all, let him eschew the Teutonic method of assigning a fundamental 'idea' to each play, supposed to have been consciously wrought out by Shakespeare, with careful introspective art. Shakespeare wrote plays for the stage, not closet dialogues for æsthetic critics. On the other hand, nothing will conduce more to a clear understanding of these dramas than carefully noting what subjects of thought were uppermost in the mind of the dramatist at various periods of his life, and great help will be found in the search for such subjects in the study of contemporaneous history, political, social, and, above all, theatrical. Sometimes more light will be thrown on the meaning of a speech or a play by a contemporaneous entry in Henslow's *Diary*, or an allusion in a work by some other dramatist, than by whole volumes of

* Is it a fancy that Shakespeare meant to illustrate one of the deadly sins in each one of the tragedies.

self-evolved comment on the ideal characteristics of *Hamlet* or *Macbeth*.

Finally, I must state my belief that no criticism of æsthetic kind is possible on Shakespeare without regard had to the succession of his works; that this succession has been obscured in the minds of critics by the division made by the editors of the folio into tragedies, comedies, and histories; that the division here suggested (following the hint of the under-rated A. W. Schlegel as to *Romeo and Juliet* and *Othello*), into plays, romantic and historical, founded on fiction and fact, treating of the individual microcosm and the body politic, is the key to the understanding of their inter-dependence.

www.ingramcontent.com/pod-product-compliance
Lightning Source LLC
Chambersburg PA
CBHW020116170426
43199CB00009B/551